This Land Is Our Land

This Land Is Our Land

THE STRUGGLE FOR A NEW COMMONWEALTH

Jedediah Purdy

Princeton University Press

PRINCETON AND OXFORD

Copyright © 2019 by Jedediah Purdy

Requests for permission to reproduce material from this work
should be sent to permissions@press.princeton.edu

Published by Princeton University Press
41 William Street, Princeton, New Jersey 08540
6 Oxford Street, Woodstock, Oxfordshire OX20 1TR

press.princeton.edu

All Rights Reserved

Library of Congress Control Number: 2019938148
ISBN 978-0-691-19564-3
ISBN (e-book) 978-0-691-19872-9

British Library Cataloging-in-Publication Data is available

Editorial: Rob Tempio and Matt Rohal
Production Editorial: Jenny Wolkowicki
Text design: Pamela Schnitter
Jacket design: Sandra Friesen
Production: Merli Guerra
Publicity: Tayler Lord and Kate Farquhar-Thompson
Copyeditor: Joseph Dahm

Jacket photo: Emmet Gowin, *Mining Exploration, Near Silver City, Nevada*,
1988. Silver print. 27.9 × 35.6 cm. (11 × 14 in.) © Emmet and Edith Gowin.
Courtesy of Pace/MacGill Gallery, New York

A New York Institute for the Humanities at NYU and
Princeton University Press publication

This book has been composed in Adobe Jenson Pro and Myriad Pro

Printed on acid-free paper. ∞

Printed in the United States of America

10 9 8 7 6 5 4 3 2 1

Contents

Preface

HOMELAND

THE SEARCH FOR A NEW COMMONWEALTH

In the years that I have been an adult, *homeland* has grown from a word Americans did not really use to a slogan by which we are ruled: in the name of Homeland Security, at once an obsessive idea and a gigantic federal agency that polices the borders, guards the president (the Secret Service), and responds to (or neglects) natural disasters (the Federal Emergency Management Agency). *Homeland* suggests a place of deep unity, where we all come from, a kind of family or at least what Robert Frost called home: the place where, when you go there, they have to take you in.

What we have now is not that. Now *homeland* is a touchstone for a divided time, when we may be marked as strangers by anything from where we live, to how we dress, to what we fear—often one another, fellow Americans. Some have more to fear than others. Ten days before I sat down to write this, officers from Immigration and Customs Enforcement (ICE) arrested Samuel Oliver-Bruno, a noncitizen who had been in sanctuary in a Durham church for nearly a year, who had left the church under pastoral escort to apply for a stay of deportation, and whose family and life had been in Durham for twenty years. I lived and taught in Durham for fifteen years, ending in the winter of 2018–19, and friends of mine were arrested while peacefully trying to stop the ICE vehicle that took him away. As I write, their legal defense is being prepared, and Oliver-Bruno is being processed for deportation in Atlanta. This is the condition of our homeland security. This land holds us together and apart, insecure.

This book's themes are how American earth has always held the people on it apart together, and how the borders at the country's edges and the borderlines that fracture "the homeland" are linked in a single web. The country began as both a world-historical land grab and a world-historical experiment in republican self-rule. The Declaration of Independence stakes its insurrectionary claim on the equality of "all men" and on the colonists' right to push their settlement beyond the Allegheny Front, where the Crown had set a border in 1763 in deference to French and indigenous claims. George Washington and Henry David Thoreau saw many things differently, but both were land surveyors. The land was the common wealth that held together the lives of presidents and dissidents in a country led to independence by its single largest speculator in land.

But despite what the commonwealths of Massachusetts and Virginia called themselves, the common wealth never became a real *commonwealth*. Instead, relations to the land formed borderlines. Colonists "justified" taking the land of indigenous people by insisting that only settlers and farmers could properly own and rule a terrain. They claimed the place with axes, plows, and surveyors' lines. From the beginning, speculative capital swelled frontier land claims in cycles of boom and bust that never really ended. Washington's will, executed in 1800, disposed of more than fifty-two thousand acres of land. Two hundred sixteen years later a minority of the country's voters elected a real estate developer as tribune of American greatness.

Land is perennially the thing we share that holds us apart. Its ownership means power for some over others, down through time from sharecroppers within living memory outside Chapel Hill to migrant laborers working in the chicken factories and hog compounds of eastern North Carolina today. Ownership is the beginning of credit, the way to turn a modest claim on the world into a grander one (the fulcrum of what is aptly called "leverage," the archimedean power that moves the world); owning nothing means having to make wealth out of your own hide. The land is sorted into those who own the places where they live, those who own another's place—like the companies that "hold" Appalachian coal and Carolina hogs and chickens (*hold*—an odd word for unembodied entities controlling the work of other hands!)—and those who work there on the sufferance of at-will hiring and firing.

This unequal power does not mean that all is animosity and alienation. It is entirely human to love a place where you are in some way bound, to find kinds of freedom and pride in a place that confines you. I know from family stories that my wife's grandfather, a union coal miner all his life (and, among other things, a grave digger when the mines weren't hiring—he knew how to make a hole in the earth), loved to be underground, loved the darkness, coolness, and closeness of the mine until black-lung disease made him too weak to work. It is human to love the thing that is killing you, and to find peace in it. Home is whatever land you have dug yourself into. But this homeland has never been a commonwealth.

Wealth comes from Middle English roots meaning "well-being" or "wellness," a condition of happiness and good fortune closely aligned with *health*. It was not until the late Middle Ages that it took on its definite sense of financial or material riches. *Common* derives from French origins meaning "shared by all." Because it is egalitarian, it has often been on the receiving end of aristocratic scorn: "common" is also low, unrefined, undistinguished, earthy. So Walter Raleigh, the courtier and double-fisted colonizer who planted migrants in Ulster and Virginia, defined *commonwealth* scornfully as a "depravation . . . the Government of the whole Multitude of the base and poorer Sort, without respect of the other Orders." John Locke, by contrast, defined it as "any independent Community," a self-governing polity that might be a monarchy, a democracy, or anything else. But there is an older sense of commonwealth that means "the general good" or the well-being of the whole community—the flourishing that is shared and open to all.

These are pretty phrases—or at least they appeal to me. But what exactly should they mean? A place to start might be what the United States has often promised and sometimes delivered to its insiders, the ones who have been counted as full members in the community: a share of the world, dignity in their work or in the condition that keeps them from working, the respect of officials and the law, the expectation that they can walk without fear or shame in any public place, confidence that they will get care when they are sick or hurt. This is an ideal of freedom in everyday activity, in work and play, that you find honorable, delightful, beautiful, worthwhile. With these quick brushstrokes I am trying to indicate the elements of well-being that a community can extend or withhold. The more widely it extends them, the more it achieves the rudiments of a commonwealth, an equality deeper than being free to lose in a hyper-competitive economy.

There is another, even deeper level to the commonwealth ideal. A commonwealth might be an economy where no one gets their living by degrading someone else, nor by degrading the health of the land or the larger living world. In such a community, the flourishing of everyone and everything would sustain the flourishing of each person. This would be a way of living in deep reciprocity as well as deep equality. The freedom of that community would not be freedom from the consequences of your actions. It would not be freedom from dependence on others, or from responsibility for them. It would be the freedom of being able to approve the results of what you do, to own your responsibilities and dependences without too much grief or resentment.

The United States is so far from being this sort of commonwealth that even trying to imagine it may seem pointless. But versions of it are the promise that leaders and prophets have made again and again, at least to those insiders who have counted as "real Americans." The commonwealth is the promise of Abraham Lincoln's 1858 claim before the Wisconsin Agricultural Society that in a democracy no one should do degrading work and everyone should have the chance to use both head and hands. (Why else, Lincoln asked, do we have both?) It is also the promise of the "cooperative commonwealth" of laborer-owners that parts of the early labor movement pursued. It's the spirit of Lyndon Johnson's 1965 plea for a Great Society "where the meaning of our lives matches the marvelous products of our labor" and the economy "serves not only the needs of the body and demands of commerce but the desire for beauty and the hunger for community." It was the radical vision that Martin Luther King Jr.'s ally Bayard Rustin advanced in the same year when he called for a second wave of the civil rights movement, "calling for public works and training, for national economic planning, for federal aid to education, for attractive public housing"—all adding up to "a security of abundance."

The American commonwealth has been blocked again and again by division and exploitation—by racism, misshapen ideas of manhood and of women, and the subtle and outright violence of owners and bosses, usually all interwoven. Much American energy—political, emotional, legal, imaginative—has gone into creating classes of people who are supposedly suited for bad work. Much has gone into making bad work that shapes the people who are pulled into it. This history—still living, still deadly, from hog farms to coalfields to places without work—can make the idea of a commonwealth seem entirely idle, a story for those are caught in what Ta-Nehisi Coates calls "the Dream," a blinkered fantasy of America as an untroubled home.

After all, the history of this continent's past five centuries is woven from fantasy on the one hand and the relentless and often inhumane and destructive extraction of wealth on the other. "The land was ours before we were the land's," the line from "The Gift Outright," which Robert Frost recited spontaneously at John F. Kennedy's inauguration (after losing his prepared Augustan doggerel in the winter sunshine and wind) is chilling in its accuracy. The dominant American claim has always been that the place belonged only incidentally to the peoples who had been here for thousands of years, and fundamentally to the settlers. As strangers, white settlers laid claim to the place.

After the land itself, the other great extraction of wealth was from the labor of enslaved people. In some southern states, a settler could claim extra acreage under state settlement laws for every enslaved person he promised to bring onto the land. The plantations of the Deep South were built by what historian Sven Beckert calls "war capitalism," the mobilization of the enslaved against the forests and swamps of the region, housed in camps far from any family, with huge death rates. The differential violence that molds white, black, and brown bodies to the concrete abstractions of race and caste is also written on the land: in how people are distributed across it, who owns it and who can imagine, after a few generations, that their people have a claim that is nearly primordial and even in harmony with the expectations of the place itself.

After the frontier came redlining. Not long ago in Durham you could map the demographics of the city across an image of the Federal Housing Authority's loan segregation maps from eighty years ago. (This has changed in recent years in a wave of gentrification, in which "color-blind" markets have replaced poorer black and Latino residents with whiter and wealthier people almost as systematically as segregation once did—albeit with more nuance and deniability.) You can spot the historically favored neighborhoods from above because willow oaks were planted along those streets eighty years ago, creating a green canopy over the white boulevards whose absence alerts you when you have crossed the old color line, giving Jim Crow an ecological echo.

This is a material story with an ecological face. For the median American household today, two-thirds of net worth is home equity. In 2015, the rate of black American home ownership was 40 percent, compared to 70 percent for white Americans. The average white household controls seven times as much wealth as the average black household, the median white household eleven times more. The land and the wealth that began in it still carry the shape of history. The chasm between white and black wealth is rooted in control of property, and it abides there. The land remembers.

But what do we remember of it? Every political contest over claims on the land is, in part, a contest over what will be remembered and what will be forgotten. With forgetting, the way things are sinks into the land itself, as if it became nature.

■ ■ ■

There are many ways to claim a terrain—by force and by the force of imagination, by cartography and by storytelling. Settlers made indigenous Americans into a kind of narrative resource, a flexible key to imagining ways of being "the land's," ways of belonging to a conquered place. Even before Thomas Jefferson's continental catalogers, Meriwether Lewis and William Clark, documented with aesthetic precision the "beautiful" and "sublime" features of the West that would later become the sacred places in American scenery, the partisan Jeffersonian poet Philip Freneau was pioneering the long literary tradition of the picturesque savage in "The Indian Burying Ground":

By midnight moons, o'er moistening dews;
   In habit for the chase arrayed,
The hunter still the deer pursues,
   The hunter and the deer, a shade!

And long shall timorous fancy see
   The painted chief, and pointed spear,
And Reason's self shall bow the knee
   To shadows and delusions here.

Freneau published these lines in the 1780s, before the U.S. Constitution was ratified, more than a century before the U.S. Army's massacre of the

Lakota at Wounded Knee. If white settlers were extracting wealth from the land before they developed any idea of how to fit into it—the less poetic rendering of Frost's line—then in poems and imagination the sequence was reversed: they were extracting the raw material of nostalgia and myth from indigenous people a century before they completed their conquest. American nostalgia and romanticism were being prepared even amid an increasingly unequal series of border wars to claim the continent. The Boy Scouts were founded in 1910 partly on the idea that young men would acquire American virtue by learning the austere disciplines and woodcraft of "little savages," in cofounder Ernest Thompson Seton's phrase. Even today a writer as thoughtful as Wendell Berry can imagine the continent's first people as living harmoniously in the "maidenhood of our world," a moral and imaginative resource for ecologists today.

This is not a morality tale. The point is not to moralize. It is a material story, an accounting of how this familiar world was made that both illuminates and rebuts the morality tales that have attached to this place. It is a story about the terms of land making that made American wealth so unequal, uncommon.

This history puts a heavy burden on the idea of an American commonwealth. It confirms that what Americans inherit in common is terribly unequal and compromised, all the way back to the first settlers who called the place by its new name (the name of Amerigo Vespucci, the Italian cartographer known for mapping it, as if we called Antarctica "Fab," for the Russian-backed explorer Fabian Gottlieb von Bellingshausen, or Australia "Jimmy" for Captain James Cook). By the same token, the history highlights why it matters that a commonwealth is not a gauzy utopian ideal: it is radical and practical. This unequal history is only prelude. The global ecological crisis that is now unfolding will grow and shapeshift for all the lives that anyone who reads this will ever know or care for, and much longer. The ways the planet has turned against us, grown smaller and angrier and more erratic, are all human creations—most of all the creations of the past and present inhabitants of North America and Europe, and now billions in China and the rest of the newly industrialized world. People whose lives are already entangled ecologically and economically will be thrown together in new ways: when refugees from storms and droughts and resource wars crash against the gates of

Europe and the United States, when one country and then another tries its own version of geoengineering on behalf of the globe. The crisis may show up, too, in new exercises of force and claims to rule. Will there be a blockade of Brazil to stop its fascist-styling government from bulldozing the Amazon and collapsing the lungs of earth's atmosphere? Will African countries with vast fertile farmland under long-term Chinese lease assert sovereignty to break the leases in a food crisis? Will New Zealanders vote to close their airports to Silicon Valley *riches* and hedge funders looking for a stable place to ride out the "end of civilization?" Already climate denialism in the United States is less about science than about who rules you: it is a way of rejecting the claims of foreigners, international institutions (more imagined than real), and the global poor, and holding on to a narrow sovereignty that the tides are threatening to wash away. The wall at the Mexican border and the Donald Trump administration's cuts in asylum for refugees are announcements that the world's problems will not be allowed to become American problems.

But that almost metaphysical American exceptionalism is a bad joke. Or, like many wild threats, it seems it must be a joke, until it turns violent. The question is not whether the world's problems will become everyone's problems, but on what terms they will. Militarized borders, resource wars, and inequality that grows as its ecological and economic faces interact: These are the features of a re-barbarized world, in which people and peoples do not even try to live in reciprocity or aim at any shared horizon beyond the ecological scarcity that presses down inequitably on everyone. The ways the world's respectable powers have been pretending to build a global commonwealth, by growth and trade, have brought us here. Although the polite official response to global inequality is still to regret it and seek ways to mitigate it, the rising political tide is a cruder and more candid call to maintain your own relatively and (temporarily) secure place in it against whoever would take it away. There is neither time enough nor world enough—we would need several worlds with comparable resources—to grow and trade our way to a global capitalist version of commonwealth. But the notorious fact that in the long run we are all dead, and so is the world, has become a perverse source of comfort to those who think they can ride out disaster long enough for their own purposes, until their own lights go out.

So there it is. To adapt an old slogan: commonwealth or barbarism. Either the world's economies turn to a new reckoning—over what is most worth doing with finite and fragile places, and with brief and vulnerable lives—or we career into a future that betrays the commonwealth idea again and again. A commonwealth politics today has to ask what wealth itself is and what is the value of life. It has to give answers that people can live by together. Otherwise we will have made ourselves one another's enemies. Fault lines and armored borders and strongmen will seem the simple necessaries of survival. If there are no commonwealth politics to bend our efforts and imagination toward, those of us who enjoy some freedom and small power in this world will have to choose between cynically hoarding a chance at half decent survival for our own families and closest allies or nihilistically watching crises crash at the walls of this unequal world, savoring the small satisfaction of having seen it coming. Neither is a way to wish to live.

Having gone briefly global, let me turn back now to the main concern of this short book: understanding the crises of American life in terms of the meaning of *this* land, the value of *these* lives, here, for the people who believe they have a homeland in this country and others who feel they live here in a sort of exile, strangers in the land—and the many of us who feel sometimes one way, sometimes the other, often both at once. I return here because, although there is need for politics on the global scale, it does not exist yet, and efforts to talk it into being are mostly vapid. If it does come into being, it will be in relation to, often emerging out of, national, regional, and local politics where feeling and power are already concentrated, articulate, able to make things happen.

The existence of problems on a global scale doesn't imply that politics must also take that scale. This is a common fallacy, so easy it can seem inevitable. But a world order can be built from an alliance of commonwealths, probably more readily than as a single, literally utopian ("no-place") commonwealth. In any event, it is easier to see that far. This book begins from what is already in common, divisive and impoverishing as it sometimes is.

The chapters that follow cross a series of landscapes. The next one, "This Land Is Our Land," explores conflicts over whose land this is, and what it means for the land to be "ours," by way of two places where nationalism and nature have come together recently: the public lands of the American West and the Appalachian coalfields, battleground of the "war on coal." "Reckonings" goes to places where the land and built environment are dangers, sources of vulnerability and repositories of harm, to consider how irresponsible and indifferent power remakes the land and the people on it. "Losing a Country" meditates on the ways that familiar places felt newly dangerous, strange, and comfortless in the winter of 2016–17, and on what it means to understand yourself as both endangered and part of the threat in a hazardous place. "The World We Have Built" draws back to consider the most consequential landscapes of the twenty-first century, the vast second nature of infrastructure and human institutions, which mutely direct the fate of the world. The final chapters, "The Long Environmental Justice Movement" and "The Value of Life," begin to map a politics for remaking the world we have built and turning the future of life toward an economy and ecology of common care.

Finally, these chapters track me from the North Carolina Piedmont, where I lived for fifteen years, to New York City, where I typed the final words in this book. In those years I got to know, and finally to identify with, a region and history different from the

ones I had known—Appalachian and Northeastern.
I walked there, voted, planted food, was arrested at the
state capitol with the Moral Mondays movement, and
came to think of my life as entangled with the life of
the place. I had the privilege of neighboring, in place
if not time, the activist, legal scholar, and priest Pauli
Murray, who has been recently "discovered" (with
a retrospective *New Yorker* profile and a Yale college named in her honor) but has been treasured in
Durham for a long time. Some days I thought I saw
Durham's Jim Crow segregated cemeteries and the
poor bottomlands where her family lived through her
descriptions of walking them as a child. With her,
I thought about how the extraordinary work that she
called a "ministry of human flourishing" could arise
from such a superficially unpromising place, one that
the writer Joan Didion had passed through as a child
with no recollection except that the other children
there ate red clay dirt from under their porches. The
discipline of living there was to see much more than
that, and this book is, among other things, a thanks
and farewell, for now, to a place where I learned new
ways of seeing. It is strange and ironic to finish these
words far from a place I learned to call home.

Acknowledgments

This book began as a lecture at the New York Institute for the Humanities at New York University, generously co-sponsored by Princeton University Press. Neither the lecture nor the book could have happened without the generous attention, support, and encouragement of Eric Banks and Melanie Rehak of the Humanities Institute, nor of Rob Tempio at Princeton. It takes many voices to make a lecture, many hands to make a book. I am grateful for all of their work.

I thank many people for conversations on the themes of this book, including Michelle Wilde Anderson, Alyssa Battistoni, William Boyd, Daniela Cammack, Jonathan Cannon, Ann Carlson, Saskia Cornes, Katrina Forrester, Michael Gerard, David Grewal, Skylar Gudasz, Matt Hartman, Django

Haskins, Olatunde Johnson, Jeremy Kessler, Madhav Khosla, Sarah Krakoff, Robert Macfarlane, David Pozen, Jessica Bulman-Pozen, Daniel Richter, James Salzman, Tehila Sasson, Isaac Villegas, Priscilla Wald, and Norman Wirzba. I am also grateful to editors who have worked with parts of these chapters along the way: Ross Andersen, Carla Blumencranz, Joseph Dahm, John Guida, Colin Kinniburgh, David Marcus, Laura Marsh, Charles Petersen, Matt Rohal, Amy Davidson Sorkin, Rob Tempio, Dayna Tortorici, Jenny Wolkowicki, and members of the n+1 editorial collective. For invitations to present some parts of these arguments in talks, I thank Tehila Sasson and Cambridge University, the Mahindra Humanities Center at Harvard University, the Yale Legal Theory Workshop, and the faculties of law at Virginia, Stanford, Duke, and Columbia. Above all I thank my wife, Laura Britton, and our family.

All writing is a memorial of intellectual debt and gratitude. I have not interrupted these essays with citations, but readers who want those and notes on further reading can find them at https://press .princeton.edu/titles/30430.html.

This Land Is Our Land

1

THIS LAND IS OUR LAND

What is the nature of our civic enmity? How do people who live together come to see one another as enemies? Not surprisingly, given the situation that makes the question urgent, there is no agreement on the answer.

There is a pastoral centrist view, still in evidence in patches of op-ed pages and short-lived presidential candidacies, that the idea of Americans being one another's enemies is a fever symptom caused by a disease called polarization. We can hope to wake up, after thrashing in the dark for a while, with cool brows and a new narrative of civic friendship in our heads.

Or maybe, instead, the enmity is a matter of some people starting to see what many others have known for a long time: that, depending on who you are, the police are dangerous, the courthouse is a menace, the official statues are civic graffiti and insults; that *la migra*, ICE, will grab and expel with one American hand the same migrants that the other hand, the economic sectors of building and cleaning and harvesting, has been beckoning and exploiting. Maybe the sense of enmity is some people's delayed awareness of what women have known for years in unsafe workplaces, and what any at-will employee knows: that a bad boss is a more immediate and intimate problem than a bad president, though the two may resemble each other and be related. Enmity may be a reminder, too, that many comfortable people have watched or overseen growing economic inequality, the hollowing out of the economic bases of whole regions and classes, and the defunding of public institutions, with only murmurs of disapproval and sympathy.

So, a question: Is civic enmity a feeling or a fact? Can a new narrative address it, or does it require abolishing what sets people at odds, whether you call that late capitalism, a rigged system, the patriarchy, coastal elitism, white supremacy, or the carceral state? I teach law, which always leaves me thinking that words and material power, narrative and force, have the closest of relations. No story or picture of the world matters much if it floats too far from what people do with one another's bodies and with soil and weapons and other tools; but also and by the same token, no material change in power will go forward without ideas and images that give it shape and a horizon to aim for. Also: the things that tie people together and the things that divide them tend to be the same things. The terms of cooperation are also the terms of exploitation and coercion. Any arrangement for living together has both sides, and they have to be understood together. How do people come to be one another's problems, threats, burdens? How do we become one another's helpers, protectors, friends?

There are many ways at this question. My starting place is the most concrete things that tie people together and also hold them apart: landscape and animal and mineral. Nature. Even the word is both unifying and dividing. *Nature* comes from the Latin root for birth, as in *natal*, the common origin of everyone. It shares that root with *native*, as in *native land*—where you were born—and so it's also aligned with *nativism*, the doctrine that ties political identity and membership to the land of your birth, and with *nationalism*, the myth that defines your people by their birth from a certain land. This myth came into the world dripping blood and soil. It claimed those as identity, sovereignty, and passport. Its stories are the beginnings of borders, just as much as rivers and coasts and ridges are.

It's a truism that nativism and nationalism are crises today. It's all too familiar that the president retails a version of true American identity in which race, religion, immigration, and the divide between coastal elites and "real Americans" all serve as boundary markers. It might not immediately seem that this nationalism has anything to do with "nature." But here, too, nationalism is bound up in American landscapes.

Consider two orders that the president issued in December 2017. They removed more than a million acres of federal land from Bears Ears National Monument and more than eight hundred thousand acres from the Grand Staircase-Escalante National Monument, both in southern Utah. The immediate effect was to open much of nearly two million acres to mining for coal and uranium and drilling for oil and gas. This was a dramatic assertion of presidential power, the first time national monuments have been shrunk in more than half a century, and the first time the president's power to shrink or eliminate monuments will be tested in court. The monument lands were in the administration's sights because they are just as controversial in southern Utah as certain other monuments in other places, such as the Confederate statue that activists took down at the beginning of 2018 in Durham and, later the same year, in Chapel Hill. Fights over monuments are also fights over whose places "public spaces" are, and who is part of any American public in the first place. The original theory of national parks and monuments was that they would exemplify the spirit of the country. They were the American cathedrals. But like some literal cathedrals, they instead attract conflict over identity that symbolically crystallizes much larger and more elusive experiences of victory and loss, belonging and alienation.

The Utah monuments came to the attention of this White House because a network of right-wing Western activists has been fixated on them. To them, the West is a colony, the federal government is an imperial power, and the public land in their counties should belong to the local public, the people who ride and hunt on it year-round and would like to have work mining and timbering it. This network connects lawmakers with lawbreakers, who turn lawbreaking into a kind of lawmaking. Ammon Bundy, who led the 2016 occupation of the Malheur Wildlife Refuge in southeastern Oregon, recently joined elected officials in San Juan County, Utah, in a local form of protest: riding four-wheelers onto public lands that officials have closed. The protestors sometimes ride armed, and not with small guns. Powerful allies in the state legislature and in Congress give the lawbreakers confidence. It was a county commissioner in San Juan, home to Bears Ears, who warned the Bureau of Land Management in 1979, when all of this was getting started, "We're going to start a revolution. We're going to get back our lands. We're going to sabotage your vehicles. You had better start going out in twos and threes because we're going to take care of you."

These claims assert local power against national power. But they are also bids for power by some local people over others. (Like nations, regions and locales are imagined communities and products of political construction.) When President Trump announced the shrinking of Bears Ears, he praised local control by people who know and love the land. That same month, a federal court ruled that San Juan County had unconstitutionally gerrymandered the county's Navajo majority into a permanent political minority in the same county government that has been lending Ammon Bundy support. Most local native political bodies endorsed the monument. The question of just *whose* land the public lands are is also a dispute over who counts in and speaks for "the public" at any level—who is treated as a real member of the political community, and on what grounds. (The meaning of being local in San Juan County may have begun to change in November 2018, when a Navajo majority entered county government for the first time.)

When Ammon Bundy was asked about the occupiers' goals in the Malheur refuge, he replied that they would be satisfied "when the people of Harney County can use these lands without fear: once they can use these lands as free men." When his occupiers began marching around public property in Oregon with pistols and rifles, it was less than a week after a police officer escaped indictment for shooting and killing twelve-year-old Tamir Rice for brandishing a toy gun. Is it unfair to pair these two American uses

of guns to lay claim to public space? I don't think so.
The pairing highlights the partiality of Bundy's version of getting free. It is not just the way American
vigilantism is racialized, so that certain white men
can pantomime unofficial communitarian violence,
or even use it, under the sign of lawfulness, while
others must use nonviolent civil obedience to appeal
to the people against the law. It is also that this claim
on land excludes other claims, asserts an exclusive
homeland, makes getting free a matter of getting
free of other people. Maybe the impulse to claim a
homeland is, among other things, a way of saying that
you do not feel at home in the world. Maybe that is
something others could recognize sympathetically,
in a different expression; but that kind of sympathy
would be saintly in response to such aggressive partiality as armed incursions and occupations, and
sainthood is no standard for civic life.

This aggressive partiality is ironically at home
on monument land. The people who created the
parks and monuments and wilderness areas also
wanted to be free of inconvenient kinds of people:
John Muir disliked and made fun of the shepherds
and laborers in Yosemite; Teddy Roosevelt and his
friends disliked and wanted to escape immigrants in

the cities; the creation of Yellowstone and Glacier National Parks meant expulsion of native people. There has never been enough public space for the contending publics who want it. The land exemplifies the country all too truly: it is the site of fights over whose country is being taken away, who is the patriot and who is the usurper or trespasser.

■ ■ ■

Now come east more than a thousand miles to the Appalachian plateau, which folds and falls over central and southern West Virginia, eastern Kentucky, and the western tip of Virginia. This land is mostly not public but private, often owned not by people who live and work there but by coal and gas corporations. The idea of civil war, which has fascinated some Americans recently, has always been close to the surface of this thin soil, where it is hard to bury anything deeply. Recently, teachers on strike for better pay and health care marched here in red bandannas to call up the history of striking workers in the mine wars that tore through this region almost a hundred years ago. More recently, in 2016 and before, the war in many people's minds was a theme of the Trump campaign, what they called the "war on coal."

The idea that environmentalists and regulators were making war on the coalfields was around as early as 2010 as a slogan of the coal industry, but it really took off when Trump's run for the presidency became a movement. When EPA director Scott Pruitt announced the repeal of President Barack Obama's Clean Power Plan, which was *the* major national initiative on climate change, he did it in Hazard, Kentucky, flanked by miners. He told them, "The war on coal is over."

The war metaphor invites some Americans to see themselves as invaded and occupied by other Americans and their illegitimate allies. In Trump's telling, this was an unjust war that suspiciously internationalist elites were waging against real Americans. In the coalfields, it was a defensive war. The miners believed they were the Resistance before the Resistance believed it was the Resistance. In this they are like the anti-monument activists, who believe they are colonized by elite easterners and bureaucrats.

War does not feel remote in the coalfields. Miners go after the land with dynamite and machines that crush mountains, remaking the terrain and hydrology of the region. And the broken land becomes a kind of guerilla enemy, poisoning streams with acid runoff and choking miners' lungs with dust that kills.

Here, too, class warfare is heritage. The "mine wars" of the twentieth century were called wars because that was what they looked like. Armies of miners tried to win a share of the world for themselves. Miners fought many times to get their unions. One failed attempt ended in the three-day Battle of Blair Mountain, where strikers exchanged hundreds of thousands of rounds of gunfire with management-backed militias and the National Guard. There is a fight now over whether Blair Mountain will be demolished for coal. When the creator of the modern United Mine Workers of America, John L. Lewis, died in 1969, union miners went out on strike for a day because that was how you mourned: by showing class power. In the same year, strikes shut down the coalfields for weeks while miners demanded a public fund to pay for their retirees' black-lung care. The "war on coal" picks up deep resonances in the region. But it replaces the old material stakes of solidarity with symbolic and rhetorical antielitism.

The phrase "war on coal" resonates because it names a feeling: being trapped in a fight with existential stakes, with no political way out. War is what we call politics that has lost its capacity to bridge, mitigate, and, most important, transform our differences. By the time the "war on coal" came along, the miners' union had been broken except as a remnant. Strikes had all but disappeared. When twenty-nine miners died underground in the Upper Big Branch Mine explosion in 2010, talk about striking for safety standards was long gone. The Waxman-Markey climate bill that failed in 2010 contained many provisions for coalfield transition. None of them struck a chord in the coalfields. Miners lived literally between a rock and the hardest place, and they did not believe that anything the government did after their jobs disappeared would repair or improve their lives. The people who wrote that legislation were not their people. A strong union might have brokered a different kind of peace, an investment in the post-coal coalfields that miners could trust as their own partial victory. It would have been expensive, but so is everything, most of all our unfolding political and ecological disaster. The problem was not that the sums were too small, but that the alienation was already too deep.

The "war on coal" language resonates with a symbolic defense of work and force—which is also to say, of a certain version of manhood. From this perspective, the environmentalists, bureaucrats, and diplomats who design climate policy may be cosmopolitan, but in a deeper sense they are unworldly. They can't handle the use of muscles and machines that tear a mountain apart to keep their screens glowing. The violence and force offend or frighten them; they couldn't do the work themselves, yet they depend on it. Celebrating mining in this vein makes the technocrats and meritocrats contemptible, and this numbs the suspicion that they run the world; it puts power and dignity back into the work miners know how to do, into the lives they know. It is a kind of symbolic revenge. Maybe in the celebration of work there is an intelligible wish to make things, to be useful, to touch and uphold and sustain the world—a wish for ways of living beyond the consumption of stimuli and of digital simulacra of social approval. But rather than any of that, we get extractivism as a political identity.

As coal becomes less important as a resource, it becomes more important as an emblem of American defiance. The defiance expresses itself as making things work—keeping the lights on; but also as tearing things up and burning them down. The blend of pride and violence, belonging and dispossession, is a thick red thread in the American manhood that figures so destructively in today's politics.

For decades, political respectables have been manipulating the language of war for initiatives that play on national divisions, like the war on drugs, and concocting new kinds of wars, like the war on terror, which can lead to real wars, like the Iraq invasion. Now it seems war is one of our major ways to talk about hanging together. And wars have more than one side. The conceit that they might have only one real side, and bring unity without conflict, existential feeling without existential stakes, is a very American thought—a certain kind of official twentieth-century American thought. It is a conceit that has escaped its masters.

■ ■ ■

This is a season of denialism. In my circles, the word tends to mean denial that climate change is real or human-caused. But denialism can stand for something broader: a refusal to see the things that tie us inconveniently together. These include the unequal history that the land remembers, the perennial presence in American life of migration and foreign labor, the decline of relative American power. You could distill it by saying that denialism is the ethos that refuses to see how the world is deeply plural at every scale *and* that we are in it together.

The denial comes not because the denialist cannot see this but because he *does* see it, not because he doesn't believe others are there but because he feels their presence so acutely, suspects they will make claims on him, fears they will get power over him and take what he has. When I was in high school in Calhoun County, West Virginia, my classmates told me that Michael Dukakis (the 1988 Democratic presidential nominee) would take everyone's guns and Jesse Jackson (who ran for the nomination that year) had a plan to put all white people in camps. Today we hear that climate change is an internationalist stalking horse for global government. Interdependence is incipient war and conquest. Climate denial is really less about science than it is about who has claims on you, and who rules you.

The denialist wants peace, but insists on terms that make peace less likely. I have been developing this idea

by talking about Ammon Bundy and alluding to a
president whose self-obsessed solipsism exemplifies
the denialist's impossible peace. But denialism has
more than one face. There is a liberal denialism, the
idea that the country just needs to get back to 2015,
that in a deep way we were doing everything right
until a monster grabbed the wheel. That thought
glides over decades of growing inequality and private debt, bleeding of industrial jobs, rising economic
precariousness, racist mass incarceration, starving
of public institutions and infrastructure, and end-
less war. It isn't just that "Republicans won't let us fix
these problems"—Democrats have been complicit in
them, or worse.

This liberal denialism makes liberals the inheri-
tors of the political culture of the Cold War—the
one many of us grew up assuming was just Time-
less America. In the 1950s and 1960s, moves
toward equality were spurred partly by competi-
tion with the Soviet Union for legitimacy in the
postcolonial world, which was not eager to honor
an apartheid state. The same geopolitical competi-
tion powered a high-minded rhetoric about how
Americans had always basically agreed on equality,

freedom, and democracy, and had just needed to work out some kinks in implementation over the years. Cold War imperatives pressed both parties to suppress their ideological flanks: the Democrats helped break the radical wings of labor, while the center-right cut ties with explicit nativism and open white supremacy. For some decades, everyone talked about the Arc of History, the Founding, the Constitution, the Better Angels of Our Nature. That language still unites Barack Obama, the late John McCain, and even Ted Cruz, who pushes his Tea Party radicalism in the language of the Founders and constitutional fidelity. But in 2016 Donald Trump short-sold the high-minded political style of the late Cold War, betting that it would buckle under pressure—that people didn't expect much from government; that a lot of voters despised their political class and the cultural and financial elites around it; and that recreational cruelty and you-can't-bullshit-a-bullshitter cynicism would feel more authentic than any appeal to better angels. Barack Obama had told us, in one of his campaign's lyrical catchphrases, that we were the people we had been waiting for. Trump intimated that we were the barbarians we had been itching for, the ones who would tear down our own decadent city.

Meanwhile, Bernie Sanders caught the wind of an insurgency whose energy also abandoned the Cold War style and treated America as the democratic left long has—not as a source of identity or a philosophical problem elaborated across generations, but as a place to be worked on, a normal and flawed country whose promise is not in its exceptionalism but in its ordinary capacity for solidarity and stronger democracy. That wind has brought a few new self-styled democratic socialists to Congress and pressed the Democratic Party toward a stronger goal of economic security, including living wages and truly universal health care. The question now is whether any party will become the vehicle of a stronger program of solidarity and common care, one that can overcome all forms of denialism. As I write, the Green New Deal has become a touchstone for progressives, while skeptics have called it unrealistic and overreaching because its advocates call for new infrastructure, technological investment, pollution controls, *and* a fight against corporate concentration and for greater social caretaking. The vision is broad and multifarious, no doubt, but to call it unrealistic for that reason is to understate the challenge. In a time when sweeping ecological crises are rooted in the very structure of the economy, and the political will to change that structure is hard to muster partly because politics is fractured and sapped by mutual mistrust, a vision of economic reengineering and renewed social solidarity is an integral part of realistic climate policy.

Thirty years after the Cold War ended, its buttresses are crumbling, and its incantations don't work anymore. In the long 1990s, which lasted from the fall of the Berlin Wall in 1989 until the financial crisis of 2008, it was common to say that, allowing for a little reform, Americans lived in the best of possible worlds. The conflicts of 2016 were a return of what had been politically repressed, reminders that the world could get much worse, yet with a new confidence in demanding that it get much better. A favorite liberal story has been that our current disaster is a crisis of norms, a loss of stabilizing political virtue that is throwing us into polarization. But deep difference and conflict, for better and worse, are the dominant historical pattern in this unequal democracy. Polarization is the historical norm. The supposed best of all worlds produced this hazardous and uncertain one. The question now is what we will do with it.

■ ■ ■

When you pull on the thread of conflicts—in Utah, in Appalachia—you find them connected with the always-fraught shaping of American landscapes and American identities. Ideas are entangled in rocks and dirt. The ground that people stand on memorializes what divides them. What kind of politics could help people to turn and face one another?

The question matters because only politics can deliberately change the architecture of shared life, change the rules and the built world that humans live in and live by. Democratic politics, in potential, creates a common space where equals have to decide the terms of their coexistence. This is hard in any version. It cannot go on well when other forces—of economics, of race, of gender—are inviting people to treat one another as subordinates, not equals. It cannot rest on heroic civic virtue. Probably it can't go on without some felt sense of the power to swing the shape of the world toward something new— better work, better play, better land. Democratic politics can survive not as a morality play, but only as a project.

This could not possibly be more important at a time when—in climate change, mass extinction, ocean acidification, soil exhaustion—the world that may be coming to destroy us is also the world we have made. And of course it isn't simply "we"—it's the effects some of us are having on the planet, unequally visited on others, through the medium of the world itself, its floods and droughts and killing heat. The natural world, the land, is the thing you can always tell lies about, because it doesn't answer—until the time you can't lie about it anymore, because it is too late.

I've talked about the what might be called Memory of the Land, how land holds the past, holds the ways it's been lived on and used. Now I want to talk about this alongside another concept, the Weight of the World. The world we've made is heavy with all the power that built it—all the literal coal firing and oil burning, and all the mastery over human time and strength, all embedded in these roads and buildings and fields and atmospheric carbon levels.

One serious estimate puts the mass of the global "technosphere," the material habitat that humans have created for themselves in the form of roads, cities, rural housing, the active soil in cropland, and so forth, at thirty trillion tons, five orders of magnitude greater than the weight of the human beings that it sustains. That is approximately four thousand tons of transformed world per human being, or twenty-seven tons of technosphere for each pound of a hundred-fifty-pound person. The world we make tells us how to live in it. If you want to stay cool in the summer and warm in the winter, communicate with others, work, feel yourself a part of the cultures in which you share, here is what you must do: enter onto these roads and rails and flight routes, tap into these power grids and data networks, use these tools infused with rare earths.

Life in the technosphere can be claustrophobic. One of the more attention-getting books to appear in recent years was a little volume by the political scientist James Scott, *Against the Grain*, which argued that the founding of cities, agriculture, literacy, government was basically a vast slave raid, in which a few entrepreneurs imprisoned everyone else in a regime of exploitation. Scott's counter-ideal, the tragic heroes of his story, is the people who were always called barbarians, living outside the city walls. I think this is so resonant now precisely because there is nothing left outside the city walls. The built world holds us inside it, and, like the natural world, holds us together, apart. The idea of being outside the walls is most appealing precisely when it's pure fantasy, when there is no outside. It's compensation for an absent wildness. The kinds of politics I've been surveying—what I've been calling denialist politics—have some of that same fantastical, compensatory character.

How might land, the base of this weighty and claustrophobic world, be involved in political reconciliation? Take Bears Ears. When President Obama created the monument, his proclamation opened with a litany of native names for the place, from Navajo, Ute, Hopi, and Zuni—all meaning "ears of the bear"—and the history of its meaning in different traditions. The proclamation also gave a council of the tribes a permanent role in governing the monument and directed the federal land agencies that have the final say to consult closely and meaningfully with the tribes. It isn't really reparation, but it's some redress for a history of expulsion and erasure—most of all because it provided a portion of power over the use and meaning of the land.

Now take the coalfields. In March 2017 the public school teachers of West Virginia settled an eight-day wildcat strike. Twenty thousand of them shut down schools in every county. They marched in red shirts and bandannas that conjured up the mine wars of a hundred years ago. The point was to remember the name of old struggles and to insist on pay and dignity for the work of social reproduction—the work of helping the human world to go on being. Our economy undervalues that work like it undervalues the natural world.

Some of the teachers in the West Virginia high school where I spent three years were splendid. More were at least diligent. But most of them reinforced the narrow yet intensely felt class divides of a small, fairly poor, and mostly white place. As a child of back-to-the-landers, lacking money and local respectability but also bookish and overarticulate, I didn't fit the local class grid, which made me acutely aware of it. I spent the ninth and tenth grades watching bright kids from poor families get punished for small infractions, slighted when they did well, and looked at askance until they made a real mistake (weed, a pocketknife pulled out in a lunch-hour scuffle) and the hammer came down. I saw these kids as bright and curious, like the often weird hippie children I'd grown up around (like me), so I saw their class not as a fact, but as something that people did to them again and again until it became real. And I saw that the people doing it to them thought nothing was happening, that the poor kids' character was just playing out the way you would, regrettably, expect it to do.

Some of those teachers sucked up blatantly to the middle-class kids. That's what happens in a place where adults are known by the status they had in high school. Class solidarity is real, and the easiest proof is in people defending their middle-class status by kicking downward, to make sure no one thinks they belong down there. So it was especially moving to me in 2018 to see teachers put down their "professional" status and stand up as people who work.

Social sustenance and ecological sustenance could become two connected ways of making peace with other people and with the living world. The teachers' strike was a reminder that making peace can start in a struggle for power. Some teachers even called for a reckoning with the coal industry. They said the companies should pay more in taxes for the wealth they take out of the state, to pay for the teaching and upbringing of people who will be living there when the coal and gas are gone. That fight over coal, the carbon capital of the industrial age, is a microcosm of the coming fights over who owns and profits from the finer, cleaner capital of mechanized production and digital platforms. The stakes are a lot alike from the coalfields to Silicon Valley. Much like a hundred years ago, a place many people think of as backward may be a frontier of the next labor movement—a movement for honoring the work of teaching, caregiving, even the work of the earth.

It is essential to this version of reconciliation that there really is something to fight over. You often hear that things aren't zero-sum. Some things aren't, but the excise tax on coal and the state's budget for teachers' pay—well, those things pretty much are. The cost of war and the cost of health care are connected in this way in each year's federal budget. The wage rate and the profit rate are connected. The land is the most concrete instance. One thing happens to Bears Ears or another, but not both: you cannot have wilderness and mining in the same place. And global ecological limits—the land writ large—are a big reason why growing our way out of these conflicts isn't enough.

What doesn't need to be zero-sum is the creation of new kinds of solidarity, new ways to feel that your good life is part of my good life, and an injury to you is an injury to me. The teachers' strike was also about

that: the teachers lined up with bus drivers and jani-
tors and coal miners, dropped a little bit of being
middle class—which means a lot in a place full of
hard and scary poverty—to join themselves to more
people.

North Carolina has a divided state government
rather than a deep-red one, a strong sanctuary
movement, and a progressive community that's
constantly engaged and cross-racial and mixes religious congregations with secular people, partly
because people there have remembered that,
125 years ago, there was a similar movement—for
both civil rights in the former plantation counties
down east and monopoly busting for the small farmers in the Piedmont. It held power in the state for
several years before an elite-led and militarized racist reaction threw it out, suppressed the black vote,
and instituted Jim Crow. The work against the new
voter suppression, for a statewide living wage, and
for defending the immigrants in your community
are all grounded partly in thinking that in that nar-
rowly horizoned place—with its segregated willow
oaks and ten-lane highways cutting through pine
flats and afternoon thunderstorms that sweep west
from the Blue Ridge and almost reliably drown your

sweltering rallies at the state capitol—in that place
solidarity is also heritage, if you can take hold of it.

So I come back to the land and the thought that it
holds people both together and apart. Its materiality,
the way it is as real as dirt, is a reminder that it *is*
something to struggle over, that nicer words and sym-
bols don't heal its hurts, even if ugly words and sym-
bols can inflame them. But it is also deeply imagined,
invested with many different actual and possible ways
of living together. The idea that it belongs originally
and essentially to everyone, that it is a commonwealth, is a horizon to bend the struggles toward.

2

RECKONINGS

The Elk River rises in the broad valleys of Pocahontas County, West Virginia, which sits across the Blue Ridge Mountains from Virginia's horse country. The Elk then spills into the narrow hollows of Webster, Braxton, and Clay counties on its way to join the Kanawha River in Charleston, the state capital. It snakes north of coalfields, through small towns built up during hardwood timbering booms. Flanked by steep slopes, it runs in shadow for much of the day. Rhododendrons, which thrive in shade, choke the narrow gorges of its tributaries. The Elk shares its thin band of flatland with two-lane roads, train tracks, and tiny camp shacks perched on the slope between the berm and the riverbank.

The last native elk in West Virginia was shot in 1875. In January 2014, the namesake river received an estimated seventy-five hundred gallons of crude MCMH, a chemical used to remove impurities from coal. It ran into the Elk from a one-inch hole in a tank belonging to a company called Freedom Industries. The leak took place a mile and a half upstream from a major intake for West Virginia American Water, a private company that provides municipal water in parts of nine counties, including Charleston. About three hundred thousand people were soon ordered not to drink their water, cook with it, bathe in it, or use it for laundry.

The spill was a reminder of the hazards of the industrial economy that simmers behind the sleek surfaces of tech and finance. In 1985, a Union Carbide plant in Charleston's so-called Chemical Valley leaked methylene chloride, sending more than one hundred people to the hospital. In 2010, twenty-nine miners died in an explosion at the Upper Big Branch mine, in Raleigh County. Mountaintop-removal mining has buried more than two thousand miles of stream headwaters and shattered hundreds of hills and mountains.

The Freedom Industries spill was another burst of industrial harm. More than a hundred people were hospitalized for symptoms including nausea and vomiting, but there were no reports of human symptoms or fish kills farther downstream where the Kanawha flows into the Ohio. Although many people in and around Charleston avoided drinking municipal water for months or longer, it turned out to be hard to say whether the harm went beyond the hassle, anxiety, and plain indignity of living without tap water. It emerged that no one knew much of anything about how MCMH affects human health. It was no one's job to know.

Under the Toxic Substances Control Act, the main federal law governing poisons, MCMH is exempt from regulation because, like more than sixty-two thousand other chemicals, it was already in use in 1976, when Congress passed the law. The safeness or danger of most of the industrial economy is opaque. We mainly ignore this reality until a large dose of some chemical ends up in a municipal water system.

The official measure of MCMH levels that determined when central West Virginia's drinking water was "safe"—one part per million—was a guess. Pretty much all that anyone knew about the chemical's health effects was what dose is fatal to rats, and that number came from a single study that wasn't peer reviewed. A crude extrapolation of this number put the fatal dose for a large adult person at a little more than two ounces. Allowing for uncertainty about the relevant differences between people and rats, as well as the extra vulnerability of the sick and aged, state officials just guessed what might be lethal for humans and reckoned from that to a dose that counted as unsafe.

It isn't as if these scantily regulated chemicals stay out of waterways most of the time. They come in at a thousand points. MCMH is part of a chemical bath that separates impurities from coal before it's burned in power plants. The resulting slurry of waste ends up in impoundment ponds, often near valley heads in former mountaintop removal sites. Sometimes the ponds flood, sometimes the dams break. Sooner or later, everything leaks.

It was, apparently, no one's job to monitor Freedom Industries' tanks along the Elk, even though state officials knew that hazardous chemicals were sitting near the West Virginia American Water intake. The West Virginia Department of Health and Human Resources had produced its most recent "Source Water" report on the site in 2002, including no reference to either MCMH or Freedom Industries.

(Pennzoil had occupied the site earlier.) The state's Department of Environmental Protection inspected the tanks in 1991, and found nothing amiss in 2010 when it responded to a report of a licorice scent, or in 2012 when it updated its air pollution oversight. The only permit issued by a state agency for the site governed storm water runoff. Local officials had asked the state legislature for new authority to plan for chemical spills, but those requests went nowhere in a state government that habitually defers to both coal and chemical companies.

On the federal level, before the spill, the Occupational Safety and Health Administration hadn't inspected Freedom Industries, and the EPA had left matters entirely to state officials. Attacking federal environmental regulation was regarded as a safe bet in West Virginia politics, a friendly gesture toward the coal side of the "war on coal." Democratic governor Earl Ray Tomblin promised, in his last State of the State address before the spill, that he would "never back down from the EPA." The state's then-junior senator, Joe Manchin, a Democrat, was elected after he ran an ad in which he pumped a bullet into a copy of the (failed) 2010 climate change bill to show his contempt for the regulation of coal. His comments on the MCMH spill avoided talk of regulation or responsibility.

The crisis was a tableau of abdication: years of privatization and nonregulation followed by panic. It was an emergency not least because inaction had ensured that no one knew enough to say that it was *not* an emergency. The response—issuing no-use orders for the water supply and mobilizing the National Guard to distribute household water—was also one of minimal government, stripped down to the military and militarized law enforcement, making up for its earlier failure to keep people safe with a show of force in the midst of an opaque crisis. A government that could have avoided the emergency would have to be much more confident and better resourced—just the kind of government the coal and chemical industries and much of the state and national political establishment were and are dedicated to blocking and tearing down.

Asked whether there should have been more oversight and emergency planning, Governor Tomblin replied as the crisis unfolded, "I'm not someone who runs West Virginia American Water." The alibi was telling. One might say that he should be, if clean water is both a human right and a collective responsibility. The crisis posed the question of who was responsible for providing one of the most basic human needs, clean and safe water, and how the public could hold them to that responsibility. The response was a portrait of a political system that had been avoiding the question.

■ ■ ■

The years that followed brought fresh reminders that environmental vulnerability is intimately involved in American inequality. In Flint, Michigan, a majority-black city whose economy has never recovered from the decline of the Detroit auto industry, lead levels in drinking water rose to twenty-six times the EPA's "safe" limit after corrosive water from the Flint River was channeled through households' lead pipes. Lead, unlike MCMH, is fairly well understood; it causes brain damage and other developmental disorders in children and can harm the nerves, liver, and kidneys of adults. The water also brought fecal contamination and, according to criminal charges filed against complicit public officials, an outbreak of legionnaires' disease that killed at least twelve people in the area in

2014 and 2015. Other officials have been charged with covering up or destroying evidence of the contamination, and the Michigan Civil Rights Commission issued a report in 2017 tracing official neglect of Flint's water to "institutional, historical, and systemic racism."

In 2016 sociologist Arlie Hochschild published *Strangers in Their Own Land*, a close study of the outlook of Tea Party supporters in Louisiana, many of whom became Trump supporters. She was interested in her informants' "deep stories"—their sense of what it means to lead a good life; what makes them proud or angry; where they feel at home. Her Tea Party friends (as she described them in the book) inhabited a region deeply polluted by petrochemical industries. One devout Pentecostal family lived on a poisoned bayou, surrounded by dead forests. They remembered that in their grandparents' time the family got much of its living from fishing and hunting in the same location, but in their parents' lifetimes cows and horses that drank from or waded into now-polluted waterways died within days. One elderly informant lost his engineering job after he was doused at work with harmful chemicals that disabled and could have killed him. Born into a Democratic family in the Pacific Northwest, he became an environmentalist after going public with stories of being ordered to dump his factory's most dangerous by-products into local wetlands, week after week, always in secret. In his eighties, he was putting up signs for Tea Party candidates. Another Tea Partier lost his home and neighborhood to a sinkhole the size of a subdivision after a risky fracking operation shattered a subterranean mineral formation (which other companies were already using to store toxic waste). Hochschild's informants knew that the chemical companies had treated their land and people badly, but they mistrusted the federal government much more. They saw it as allied with people who wanted to "skip the line" of the American dream, a kind of "cheating" that they associated with affirmative action, government paychecks, and unauthorized immigration. They saw themselves as hardworking, patient, realistic people who understood that you sometimes have to damage the land to pull wealth from it. Race ran silently but powerfully through this story: the line-skippers were easy to imagine as nonwhite, and Hochschild's informants were almost all white. These "deep stories" also showed something you might call a tribalism of institutions: having decided that government was the ally of the line-skippers, Hochschild's people identified fiercely with government's opposite, the "free market," which in practice meant the companies that had hired them, abused some of them, and desolated their woods and bayous. One of several warlike features of recent American politics is the willingness to suffer at the hands of the institutions your people identify with, and to forgive them nearly anything out of loyalty. Hochschild's Louisianans were partisans of the market, fighting and sometimes dying in its trenches, its own private patriots.

Two years later, journalist Eliza Griswold published *Amity and Prosperity*, a report from the fracking fields of Washington County, Pennsylvania, on the fringe of Appalachia. Named (in bleak irony) for two towns that sit near each other in the county, the book is woven around the stories of Stacey Haney, a nurse and divorced mother of two, and her sister, Shelly, who for most of the book is a single mother. Stacey is an anti-fracking activist by accident. Her political work emerges from years of frustration trying to persuade state and federal regulators and Range Resources, the local fracking behemoth, to acknowledge and do something about the slow poisoning of her family by contamination from fracking fluids. Their landscape is both postindustrial and pastoral, with a patchwork of small, cash-poor farms overlying miles of abandoned mines. Their water supply is often drained off underground when wells flood into old mine shafts. Streams are sometimes dangerously polluted, thanks partly to a local entrepreneur who makes his money illegally dumping toxins. There were once steel jobs—Pittsburgh is not that far away—and the Haneys' father, a Vietnam vet with posttraumatic stress disorder who lost his mill job under Ronald Reagan, feels permanently betrayed by American geopolitics and industry. The fracking boom brings a new industrial army into Washington County—Texans, Oklahomans—and the young men in pickups bring the fights, prostitution, and drug use of all boom towns.

Griswold shows clearly, without needing to get theoretical, how closely economic powerlessness is tied to the incapacity to control your environment, or even to make confident sense of it—your interpersonal environment, to be sure, but first of all your physical environment. Being rural and working class in her book is a series of bodily situations:

contaminated water, children with chronic pain and fatigue, and no money or extra time to address the fact that their grades are collapsing year by year. It is living downhill of the pond where fracking fluids are stored. It is being hurried through a signing session for a drilling lease on your small property, without a lawyer and without a chance to read documents written to confuse you. It is wondering whether you have time to meet with an environmental enforcement agent about your problems when the last one disappeared without communicating and every meeting means time away from your nursing job. It is lawyers and bureaucrats looking at their phones while they meet with you, without apologizing. It is a high-schooler adjusting his expectations from going to college to joining the Army to mowing lawns.

It is months of scrimping to keep up appearances at the 4-H livestock show, while your ailing son would rather smoke weed than promenade for the judges with his goat, and it is the mix of gratification and humiliation when the fracking company you are fighting buys the children's animals at the subsequent auction—traditionally a compliment, but now also a way of saying they own you. It is wondering what God is trying to tell you when thieves—you assume they are junkies, because most property crimes near you are committed for drug money—strip the house you have abandoned because of contamination. In short, it is doing your very best, working hard and showing up, and learning that no one is paying attention, and that the world is not set up to reward you or even to make sense to you.

My father's family farmed just north of Washington County, on the other side of Pittsburgh, for nearly two hundred years. When I read Griswold's story, I hear familiar echoes in the speech of her characters, locutions that strike her as exotic, such as "the roof needs fixed," which come naturally to me though I have learned to hear them as not quite proper. When I read her descriptions of a family that cannot keep industrial contamination out of its water, its basement air, its bloodstream, I also think of the history I learned in my fifteen years in Durham. As I mentioned earlier, one of this town's prized children is Pauli Murray, the legal scholar, activist, and priest who influenced Thurgood Marshall and Ruth Bader Ginsburg, who became the first black woman ordained in the Episcopal church, who loved women and did not feel entirely at home in her female body and, in the mid-twentieth century,

was scarcely able to find public words for that experience. Her memoir of growing up in Durham
details a landscape of unequal vulnerability. Like
many black Durhamites, her family lived in "the bottoms," the downslope flats where small, dirty creeks
flood when summer thunderstorms, fall hurricanes,
or winter rains saturate the red-clay soil. Murray's
childhood home was just downhill from a grand,
then-segregated cemetery that still occupies acres
of land a short walk from Duke University's cam-
pus. In rains, she recalled, the water that poured into
the lawn and flooded the family garden came down
from the white graves up the slope. It was as if other
people's deaths filled the soggy bottom and made
it not the Murrays' own, left them with no home
they could shape in their own image. The caste systems of race and class in this country have always
been shaped by unequal answers to some of the oldest questions in human settlement: whose waste is
carried away, invisible to them, and who carries and
absorbs it? Who can control the boundaries of their
own land and water, and finally the boundaries of
their bodies, and who is always susceptible to per-
meation, or ends up being treated as matter out of
place, a kind of human pollution? Where I grew up

in West Virginia, environmentalists would remind one another, "We all live downstream." That lesson of the ecological age is the possible starting point for a new politics of deep reciprocity, but also a spur to a new chapter in the age-old scramble for safety on high ground, where no one can reach you.

■ ■ ■

Power rearranges people on the land. Those who cannot control their environment are controlled by it. The gas-field roughnecks who showed up around Amity and Prosperity (finding a few years of the second, if none of the first) are just as much emblems of the age as the locals whose lives they disrupted. Like the other commodities of the energy economy, wage laborers are sometimes defined less by any place they call home than by their patterns of movement. They are drawn from the land in one place, run through factories in another, and processed in the massive logistics hubs of ports, rails, trucking networks, and warehouses. This is called labor-market efficiency, and some forward-looking thinkers have suggested the duties of social justice end at paying dislocated farmers and miners to join in it by moving their lives across the land. In global value chains, much of the land is organized by these patterns of capital-dictated movement, sorted into what geographer Phil Neel calls "hinterlands," the invisible but indispensable logistics hubs where the shitty but abundant jobs are—the Amazon warehouses of the world, and many lower-tier centers of production and transfer—and the increasingly depopulated countryside of extraction and primary commodity production where jobs in farming, mining, and logging are being lost to automation, and not much has shown up to replace them. These are the little towns where militias crop up, the places that went 60 and 70 and 80 percent for Trump in 2016. There are such landscapes everywhere because production, extraction, and other work reflect the same logic. The same warehouses and heavily mechanized factories spring up in depopulated fields and forests, and little towns everywhere are emptied of working-age people, leaving the same desolate hinterlands. In the decade following the financial crisis of 2008, virtually none of the return of work and growth took place in small towns or rural counties, with the destructive and transient exception of the fracking boom.

Who will they and their children be, the people who do the logistics work, taking orders from algorithms to keep global markets humming? What about the ones who have not even been able to get jobs in this economy—left-behind people in left-behind places, getting by on the peripheries of the deep hinterland? Neel points out that even as "whiteness" is being elevated as an identity on the alt-right and interrogated on the progressive left, its material reality is increasingly fragmented. The chiefly white professional and "upper-middle" classes thrive, while statistics show rural and blue-collar whites slipping toward unemployment, imprisonment, and early death. These fates still inequitably affect African Americans, Native Americans, and Latinos; but, given the depth of racial inequality in the United States, it surely reveals an important shift in lines of vulnerability that, in at least thirty counties in the South, middle-aged white women are dying faster than black women of the same age. Even as race and racism become more salient in national politics, the disregarded and discarded classes are a composite of the downwardly mobile and the long trapped, who often remain scared of one another despite an increasingly shared situation in the economy that makes their lives.

At the same time, ironically, a southern-inflected "country" culture has become the standard fare of white Trump voters, who are mostly exurban and middle class but are drawn to the touchy toughness of the big truck, the rifle, and the swagger. "Country" style generally, a form of distinctly white identity that spans exurbs and rural places, is a weird mix of western kitsch and southern threat—cowboy boots and Confederate flags in the northern Midwest and western New York, places once better known for radical miners' unions and abolitionism.

■ ■ ■

Power changes the land, turns it from one place into another. So coal has remade central Appalachia. At its peak in the mid-twentieth century, mining employed more than 150 thousand people in West Virginia alone, mostly in the state's rugged and otherwise poor counties. For decades, the United Mine Workers of America, a muscular, strike-prone union that allied itself with Franklin Roosevelt in supporting the New Deal, anchored the solidly Democratic highlands where West Virginia meets eastern Kentucky and Virginia's westernmost tip. Today, after decades of mechanization, there are only about twenty thousand coal miners in West Virginia, and another sixteen thousand between Kentucky and Virginia. The counties with the greatest coal production have some of the region's highest unemployment rates, recently between 10 and 14 percent. An epidemiological study of the American opiate overdose epidemic found two epicenters where fatal drug abuse leaped more than a decade ago: one was rural New Mexico, the other coal country.

Although jobs have disappeared, Appalachia keeps producing coal. Since 1970, more than two billion tons have come from the central Appalachian coalfields. West Virginians mined more coal in 2010 than in the early 1950s, when employment peaked at nearly six times its current level. Back then, almost all coal miners worked underground, emerging at the end of their shifts with the iconic head lamps and black body paint of coal dust. In the 1960s, mining companies began to bulldoze and dynamite hillsides to reach coal veins without digging. This form of strip mining, called contour mining, caused more visible damage than traditional deep mining, leaving mountains gouged and farmland destroyed.

Today, contour mining seems almost artisanal. Since the 1990s, half the region's coal has come from "mountaintop removal," a slightly too-clinical term for demolishing and redistributing mountains. Mining companies blast as much as several hundred feet of hilltop to expose layers of coal, which they then strip before blasting their way to the next layer. The giant cranes called draglines that move the blasted dirt and coal stand twenty stories high and can pick up 130 tons of rock in one shovel load. The remaining rubble, called overburden, cannot be reassembled into mountains. Instead, miners deposit it in the surrounding valleys. The result is a massive leveling, both downward and upward, of the topography of the region. According to Appalachian Voices, an advocacy organization, mining has destroyed upward of five hundred mountains.

The Appalachian coalfields were formed from swamps that, 310 million years ago, covered the region. Some quarter of a billion years ago, tectonic forces thrust the region upward to form a plateau, which has been since shaped mainly by erosion. Accordingly, its landforms are folded around waterways. Place names reflect this: Alum Lick, Barren Creek, Frozen Run, Left Hand, Stone Branch. The webs of trunks and tributaries form one half of the spatial logic of the region, alongside the ridges that split them into watersheds. A walk that would take miles along creek bottoms is a quick, if arduous, scramble over a ridge. A misstep descending from a ridge can put a walker in the wrong hollow, following an unforeseen stream.

Although precise tallies are elusive, Environmental Protection Agency reports suggest that valley fills have buried over two thousand miles of "headwater streams," the small, sometimes intermittent flows through leafy forest floors and rhododendron groves where waterways pick up nutrients and other organic matter that supports life downstream. In 2011, the EPA estimated that mining had altered 7 percent of the surface area of the central Appalachian coalfields. In 2012, it reckoned that 1.4 million acres of native forest had been destroyed and was unlikely to recover on the broken soils that mining leaves. A 2016 study attempted a landscape-scale accounting of the transformation of Appalachia. Using detailed satellite data for a 4,400-square-mile portion of southeastern West Virginia, it describes a terrain that has been broken and transformed. Active and abandoned mining sites occupy 10 percent of the region. In those sites, rubble fills valleys to depths of six hundred feet. Blasting and bulldozing have lowered ridges and mountaintops by as much as six hundred feet as well. A steep terrain with sharp contrasts between high ridges and low, stream-cut bottomland is becoming a broken and strewn average of its original topography.

Where it has not been ground down by mountaintop removal, Appalachia is a region of slopes. There is precious little level ground aside from narrow ridgelines and narrower hollows. In the 10 percent of the study area that has been mined, a terrain dominated by steep hillsides has been replaced by a mix of plateaus and remnant or reconstructed hillsides that are shorter and blunter than before mining. The most common pre-mining landform was a slope with a pitch of twenty-eight degrees, about as steep as the upper segments of the cables of the Brooklyn Bridge. Today, the most common is a plain with a slope of two degrees, that is, level but uneven. Across the entire study region, mining has filled a steep landscape with pockets of nearly flat ground. Researchers estimate conservatively that the volume of central Appalachian earth and rock turned from mountain to valley fill is equal to the amount of ash and lava that spewed from the Philippines' Mount Pinatubo in 1991, about 6.4 billion cubic meters. For comparison, that is thirty-two times the volume of material that the 1980 Mount St. Helens eruption deposited in the northern Cascades.

The region's hydrology has been remade. Because streams begin on mountainsides, and it is mountains that are being mined, the region's headwaters have been transformed. In place of mountains formed from solid rock and coal, with a thin layer of dirt at the surface, there are now deep sinks full of compacted rubble, which works as a sponge. Researchers calculate that the valley fills can hold a year's worth of rainfall, ten times more than the thin, clay-rich pre-mining soils can hold.

As water lingers in the porous fills, it takes up chemicals from shattered rock. It also absorbs alkalinity from carbonate stone that mining companies deliberately mix into overburden to stop the broken stone from producing acidic runoff, which has turned many streams in mining regions bright orange and lifeless. But the cure is its own poison. Streams emerging from valley fills are as much as an order of magnitude more alkaline than neighboring flows. They also show high levels of toxic selenium, released from stone by mining. The streams are not dead, unlike those in watersheds killed by acid runoff, but the mining pollutants reduce fish and plant life well downstream of the valley fills.

■ ■ ■

Coal is the cheapest source of energy, economically speaking, and the most costly in ecological terms. Its carbon emissions are the highest of any energy source. In 2012, coal accounted for 25 percent of American greenhouse gases and 44 percent of global carbon emissions. In the past few years, atmospheric carbon has continued its upward climb and as I write is at about 412 parts per million. It was only around 1990 that it passed 350 parts per million, the number scientists have converged on as the threshold of potentially catastrophic climate change.

Twice, in 1999 and 2002, federal district courts in West Virginia found that valley fills violated legal duties to protect streams. In 2001 and 2003, the federal appeals court in Richmond, Virginia, reversed those decisions, allowing valley fills to go forward. During the decade that followed, about half of America's electricity came from coal, while

China's boom raised global coal demand much as it raised prices for other industrial building blocks, such as steel and concrete. A gift from the Mesozoic to the Industrial Age, source of London's pea soup fogs, and platform of violent labor strikes decades before the New Deal, coal can feel anachronistic in the twenty-first century. It powered an older generation of iconic factories—the steel mills of Gary and Aliquippa—and a fading kind of community among workers. Miners' unions were the spine of the British Labor Party and arch-Democratic Appalachia. Recently the remnants of these towns and villages voted heavily for Donald Trump and for Brexit.

Coal, more than any other fuel, does harm where it is burned and where it is dug. And geology is forever, at least compared to the lives of people and nations. Many other environmental harms recede in a human lifetime as toxins disappear and ecological health returns. After Congress passed the Clean Water Act in 1972, waterways that had been devastated by pollution recovered rapidly. Lake Erie and the Hudson River still hold massive toxic deposits in their silty bottoms, but their fish and plant life have returned, and they are officially open for swimming. Even coal's killer fogs pass and take with them acid's erosion of statues and buildings. But Appalachian streams will be flowing from the broken, heaped stone of valley fills for millions of years.

Because mountaintop removal's harms go so deep and last so long, they make archaic-feeling coal an ironic emblem for "the Anthropocene," our planetary epoch, when humanity has become a force in the development of the planet. Both mountaintop removal and climate change, the iconic crisis of the age, are geological, changes in the chemistry and physical structure of the earth. Both tell us that we are no longer just scratching the surface, but instead working our changes very deep, where they will not come out soon. The remaking of the Appalachian landscape, which has moved so much ancient carbon from underground into the planet's fast-heating atmosphere, is a tractable lesson in the way that this global upheaval is formed of many smaller upheavals and ruined places.

3

LOSING A COUNTRY

By now, in my forties, I have a memento-box full of political losses. Durham, 2004: I have been working the polls all day for John Kerry, riding a wave of energy among voters who tell me we are going to end the war in Iraq. Someone who knows someone who knows everything has called my cell to say that Kerry's lead in the exit polls is a sure thing. I am bobbing like a buoy in a freshet, speeding over one of Durham's many snaky tangles of elevated highway, when my car's CD player shuffles up the first mournful notes of Johnny Cash's rendition of Trent Reznor's "Hurt." In my magical-thinking mind, I know Kerry has lost and spend the rest of the evening waiting for the confirmation. Such scenes go back to 1980, when my six-year-old self labored to absorb the news that my family was at odds with its country, personified in Ronald Reagan. All of this is offset by a golden morning in November 2008, which I began in Durham and ended in New Haven, passing through Harlem's 125th Street train station on my way to teach after days of canvassing. It was an uncannily beautiful and gentle day, as if the light were passing through a curtain of richly colored dried leaves, and the air on the streets was of carnival. I felt my walk might turn into a dance, and any fleeting smile into a high-five or a hug. (The man who checked in my rental car at six that morning came around the counter to hug me the moment I half-hinted that I was unrested because I was happy.)

But nothing has hit me quite like 2016. The American political calendar creates a hiatus between elections and their consequences. The nearly two months from early November until January 20 is a sort of penitentiary, in the old sense: a time of confinement in which to consider what we have done, or, depending on your standpoint, what has befallen us. That season was especially bewildering after Donald Trump won the presidential election, thanks to the Electoral College, the antidemocratic constitutional quirk that gave the victory to the candidate with three million fewer votes than his opponent. As I had in

2004, but over a longer time, I had allowed myself the comforts of magical thinking in the summer and fall of 2016. Although I would have said that I knew better, I halfway accepted the assurance that Trump's victory, while an intense thing to contemplate, was impossible in the end—impossible because it was so difficult for me and many of the people around me to imagine. (This was the mood of fall 2016, as if a large asteroid were passing within a few million miles of the earth—catastrophe glimpsed, but fundamentally at a safe distance. As that fall recedes, more and more people tell me that they expected the result. I want to see proof, since so few of them said it then.) Once the votes were counted, the asteroid had struck, I was shaken by the question: What else is possible? Not just theoretically possible, but maybe on its way to happening, that I have not really imagined? What else have I failed to understand about this place?

In that state of mind, I stumbled across a passage of Henry Thoreau's from 1854: "I have lived for the last month ... with the sense of having suffered a vast and indefinite loss. I did not know at first what ailed me. At last it occurred to me that what I had lost was a country."

Thoreau was responding to Massachusetts's enforcement of the Fugitive Slave Act to return Anthony Burns to a slaveholder from Virginia. Despite the distance in time and setting, the phrase seemed to hand back to me my own disorientation. I had a few days off at Thanksgiving, and although I had meant to go on working at the sleepless pace that had kept me feeling purposeful for nearly three weeks past the election, I was suddenly too sick to move. (Other adults with careers, responsibilities, children, described similar illnesses, sooner after the vote: days of crying, throwing up, not getting out of bed.) I began reading Thoreau's journal from the time that he was writing that essay (which he called "Slavery in Massachusetts"):

June 17, 1854: "Another remarkably hazy day; our view is confined, the horizon near, no mountains; as you look off only four or five miles, you see a succession of dark wooded ridges and vales filled with mist." That summer, to observe nature was to meet opacity and obscurity, in which it was hard to see and hard to think.

Often, in the second and third weeks of November, I trusted only the days when the sun did not come out at all; just enough light seeped through the clouds to make the streetlamps go dark. Bright days felt deceiving. They even reminded me of a bright, perfect morning in September fifteen years earlier, when a friend's phone call had alerted me that the World Trade Center was on fire. When I admitted this crazy-seeming thought, more than one person told me I was not alone in it.

Thoreau continues, "I walk toward one of our ponds; but what signifies the beauty of nature when men are base? The remembrance of my country spoils my walk.... My thoughts are murder to the state." Where the same passage appears in the journal, he adds, "I endeavor in vain to observe nature."

He was describing a mind under pressure, flattened and interrupted by outrage, lies that became law, laws that became facts, and facts that, uncontested, became the truth. This man, Anthony Burns, the law called a slave, and he was going back to one Mr. Suttle in Virginia as the Constitution required. Losing a country meant, for Thoreau, seeing these moral lies become legal and physical facts, knowing they were made in his name because he was part of the political power that made them.

Losing a country might mean losing whatever accommodation you had made with the country, losing your way of living with it. The country has not receded far away, but grown overwhelmingly close. It occupies your head in the most disruptive and intolerable ways.

A country lost in this fashion may never have been more than a pleasing illusion, a gauze of selective ignorance or indifference. "Losing a country" may be a way of describing coming to see it more clearly. To use a phrase that is facile but also necessary, Thoreau is complaining about, among other things, losing the privilege of ignoring slavery much of the time while also disapproving of it. And to be able to make this complaint publicly, to report on your new and unsettling experience of citizenship, is also a part of privilege. Anthony Burns, whose reflections in the Boston courthouse are not recorded, knew a great deal about the United States, and it seems likely that in his mind he had no country to lose. (Thoreau understood this: Amid the crisis induced by John Brown's attack on Harper's Ferry, he began an antislavery address to twenty-five hundred listeners at Boston's Old North Church by announcing, "The reason why Frederick Douglass is not here is the reason why I am"—a phrase whose snapping specificity could redeem the entire genre of the privilege check.)

But like many progressives who show up for die-ins and Black Lives Matter vigils and Moral Mondays mass arrests, I am much more Thoreau than Burns. I did not exactly believe that this country, with its extremes of wealth, poverty, and insecurity, its racial resentments and racial terror, was "already great" in Hillary Clinton's meant-to-be reassuring sense. But I did have a country to lose.

Having lost it, I wandered at the beginning of what already seemed certain to be four years of vigils, civil disobedience, encryption, surveillance, and the tiring reassertion, every day, of basic facts against lies that had become almost official. It was clear from the start that Trumpism depends on the kinds of mental disruptions that Thoreau describes. It locks the attentive citizen into the unrelenting present of the president-elect's all-hours social media feed, like the oracular communiqués of a deranged minor god. Well-meaning Facebook friends urge us to watch the cabinet appointments and ethics breaches behind the tweets, but it is never satisfying to say, as they do, that the tweets are a distraction, a smoke-screen. They are that, but they are also a mode of governance, a minor form of official entertainment and a soft, plausibly deniable mode of state terror.

Ignoring them feels—to me, anyway—irresponsible; but following along presses you out of the moment, bends your mind toward some terrible future that may never come or may already be here. "Is this the beginning?" you ask, though you wish you weren't asking. Is this how it starts?

Events were already filling up the hiatus in the winter of 2016–17, cabinet appointments populating the blank spaces where speculation was frantically sketching disasters. But now, when that winter is disintegrating into memory, there may be something to learn from the bewilderment of that season, something about finding ways across a newly disorienting landscape.

Thoreau treated both solitude and social life with utter seriousness because he believed both were at once necessary and impossible. Alone, you were in the company of received ideas, condescending self-judgment, anxiety that you were not doing your part; in company, you were alone in your strange mind— and everyone's mind is strange—throwing words like stones into the pools of other people's minds, disturbing their smooth surfaces. No wonder he wanted words that had life in them. No wonder he said the great miracle would be to see through another's eyes for a moment. He repeated that drama of recognition with his pond, imagining himself asking of the deep pool, "Walden, is it you?"

I was hungry not to be alone. I was hungry, too, for naïve responses to nature. In those days, when I saw a flock of birds wheeling in synchrony, I felt as if a dimension of awareness had opened that was not occupied territory. I felt this other site of consciousness, this fast-banking collective intelligence in its silhouette pattern, as a rip in the curtain that events had drawn between the world and me.

Thoreau's responses to nature are not naïve, but they do not reject what is alive and instructive in the naïve response. And there has been a certain value in naïveté in these years—not simple naïveté, but a kind of second naïveté that one returns to after time away. There can be a recovery, at the center of a mostly necessary labyrinth of equivocation and qualification, of something nonnegotiable. The nonnegotiables have included the rejection of religious bigotry that sent many of us racing to our local airports to protest the president's "travel ban" in the winter of 2017 and the rejection of sadism at the border that has drawn protestors to detention centers and to the cruel, empty deserts that the government trusts to be landscape-scale weapons against migrants—unless covert helpers get them water, shade, and food. These gem-hard points of humanitarian solidarity are not enough to make a politics, but they do matter. Not the most important thing about them, but not the least, is that they are a place to stand, a refusal to let everything go up for negotiation or get lied out of existence.

One of the liberal slogans of the 2016 election was that while you can choose your own opinions in politics, you cannot choose your own facts. This turns out not to be straightforwardly true. In politics, you can propose your own version of the facts and, if you win, set to work imposing your chosen facts on everyone else. That is the remaking of lies into law and into facts that overpowered Thoreau's attention in the spring of 1854. It is why the misinformation in the president-elect's tweets—for instance, the lie that millions of people voted illegally for his opponent—is not laughable and does not weaken him. Each political lie is a bid to remake reality, whether by "justifying" voter disenfranchisement or by building up the suspicion that some people's votes do not really count because they are not real Americans.

It was a "maimed and imperfect nature" that he was "conversant with," Thoreau wrote in his journal, and the insight in that phrase makes his claim to converse with nature credible. Walking to the ponds, as he put it, was never a return to something pristine. It was, like politics, a way of joining in with a record of damage, and of conceits and fantasies turned to material facts. Consider any American landscape: the Midwest, a surveyor's grid of corn and soybeans; the Deep South, a plain first cleared for planting by gangs of enslaved people marched across the land from the old colonies; the Appalachian coalfields, whose severe slopes, narrow ridges, and valleys are being transformed by mountaintop removal into a broken, spongy, uneven plateau. Even places made for respite, parks and wilderness areas that advertise "natural beauty," are legally enshrined geographic testimony to a painterly ideal of American paradise. So to reencounter nature, after losing your way in your own country, would never be an escape from history and social life into a greenwood idyll. It would be a way of getting another angle of vision on the same social facts, the same greedy and unequal humanity. Although the phrase comes from Marx rather than Thoreau, it would mean seeing in a landscape the nonhuman body of the species, in which the history of economic and political life is written as vividly as in laws. That is not comforting, but it is clarifying.

Seen clearly, nature and landscape are palimpsests of history and social violence more than they are respites from these things. They show back to the observer the durability and definiteness of the world people have made so far, as well as its fragility. In my mind at least, thinking in response to terrain, as Thoreau always tried to do—and sometimes found, in the grip of politics, that he could not—can support a kind of political clarity, an alternative to the hopeless way in which the world runs away from us but still will not let us go. It can propose a vantage point.

I realized some time ago that a vantage was what I was after in dreams of landscapes that recurred for several years. In these dreams, I started out walking up a wooded slope, and—departing from the low terrain of the Carolina Piedmont where I lived then—the slope rose through the loblolly pine into steep pastures. The pastures leveled out into high meadows, then rose again to crests of stone. Sometimes the terrain was more modest; there was no stone, just meadows at the top, sloping along a broad ridgeline. Sometimes a few hundred vertical feet of pasture made the highest landform in the dream, tufted with black oak and shagbark hickory.

Only waking destroyed my new geography. The dreams felt so real that more than once I looked up topographic maps, just to see whether the hills were really there, quietly looming over the surrounding Piedmont. Their place on the local terrain was definite. I could point to precisely where the loose, fat topo curves of the gently varying Piedmont should have drawn together to mark the steep rise that I had dreamed.

These dreams might seem to belong to the genre of the hidden room. In hidden-room dreams, a familiar house, maybe a childhood home or college dorm, opens up at the back or through the attic to reveal new spaces: grand parlors, ballrooms, greenhouses, formal lawns, interior pools. The idea that strange worlds wait behind a quotidian portal seems to be perennial, and it enchants the world. The portal is C. S. Lewis's wardrobe, Madeleine L'Engle's tesseract, the Tardis, the terrifying upside-down of *Stranger Things*, and, of course, Platform Nine and Three-Quarters. Probably it shares an imaginative

root with the afterlives and other worlds that many
cultures have supposed thrived underground.

The hidden room charms me, too, but I have been
thinking of my landscape dreams a little differently.
I think now that the wish these dreams express is
for a way to get above a terrain without leaving it, to
merge many small horizons into one image. These
dreams sketch a geography of thinking, a way of seeing a place whole without being overcome by it.

Of course my dream landscape is not the only geography of thinking. It is the one that you might
carry if you had grown up where I did, in a very specific Appalachian landscape. From any place that
people lived, you could escape on foot to a higher
spot: every settled place contained its own upward
exits. Such a landscape gives its dissidents a path to
escape on foot, at least for a while, and lends them
a commanding view of the lowland. Imagining it is a
try at remaking a kind of thinking that recent events
have threatened to rip away in the distraction, fear,
and opacity that come with having the mind occupied
by very bad politics.

This is a deliberately personal way of talking about
paths out of, or through, the dark wood where some

of us woke up on November 9, 2016, and have been wandering since. But it is not a new or unusual thought that ways of relating to the natural world would be connected with ways of navigating politics, or that the link might be especially important in times of bafflement and fear.

In 1727, an unusually hot summer in Boston was followed by an earthquake that Cotton Mather described as "a horrid rumbling like the sound of many coaches together, driving on the paved stones with a most awful trembling of the earth." Thomas Prince, the Harvard-trained minister of Boston's Old South Church, told his parishioners: "When [God] has a mind to show it, he can easily and in a moment . . . affright the hardiest creature. He can put all nature, even the great and inanimate parts of the world into such a commotion, as to make us see in a most sensible manner, the terrifying actings of his powerful presence, and excite the highest and most awful reverence of him. He can make the heavy and dull earth to tremble . . . as if it were moved with the fear of its present destruction." Thomas Prince's God had the tactics of a terrorist, or a midnight tweeter with both a nation-state and vigilantes behind him, dealing out spectacular reminders that no place was safe. In England, too, in that century and the one before it, monarchists and "natural theologians" replayed the ancient argument that fear was spontaneous proof of divine authority. Even atheists were scared of thunder and lightning, argued Henry More, the Restorationist philosopher, and this showed that all rebellions against established power were fragile and juvenile vanity. Nature underwrote authority, and fear was its imprimatur.

There was another ancient tradition, associated with the philosopher Epicurus and the Epicurean poet-philosopher Lucretius, whose thought was recovered and widely circulated in the fifteenth and sixteenth centuries. This tradition was radical and therapeutic: it aimed to get at the root of the fear that Thomas Prince and Henry More celebrated and to disentangle it from the metaphysics of thunderstorms and the political theory of earthquakes. Fear and anxiety were rational and inescapable in a dangerous world, argued Epicureans. Those who took essential hints from Lucretius were as diverse as the grim political logician Thomas Hobbes and the sensual essayist Michel de Montaigne.

The errors of fear, according to the Epicureans, included imagining that earthquakes and diseases had a moral or taught a lesson; imagining that power and hierarchy were somehow natural and ordained; believing in theological principles that obliged you to kill or torture another person; believing in a bright boundary between civilized people and barbarians, us and the others, that would justify you in ignoring their suffering, or even license you to enjoy it. When you began to interpret the world this way—or, more likely, allowed ideologues and theologians and rulers to interpret it for you in these ways—you felt your fear assuaged by a spurious order. But really you were in a greater danger than you knew, and you had become more dangerous to others, too.

Hobbes believed the solution was a relentless disenchantment of nature. We could free ourselves from deranging fear by seeing the world as matter in motion, nothing more. Montaigne, who made pleasure a central theme of his writing, argued instead that it was possible for a kind of humane and egalitarian affection to flow between people and the nonhuman world. He wrote about what he called "a general duty of humanity" that attached "not only to animals, who have life and feeling, but even to trees and plants. . . . There is some relationship between them and us, and some mutual obligation." He was describing a disposition of feeling and imagination, a cultivated openness to the multiplicity of one's own emotion and experience, of nonhuman life, and of human character and action. "The most barbarous malady of all," he wrote, "is to despise one's own being," and it was people who did, who could not control their own fear and disgust, who went seeking barbarians to torture and animals to slaughter, and so became barbarians themselves.

At the moment, the same political forces that are trying to convince us that we face barbarians at the national borders, barbarians who have infiltrated the country as refugees, and barbarians in a global war of civilizations between so-called Judeo-Christian capitalism and Islamic fascists—are also trying to convince us that we have nothing to fear from climate change. Here, the historical sides have switched. It is liberal rationalists who tell a story about the moral and political meaning of the weather, and it is the hierarchical and nationalist conservatives who deploy the little knives of skepticism. If climate politics and policy fail, it will not be because of one massive and candid refusal, but by a thousand skeptical cuts, convenient equivocations, and rationalizable delays.

The Trumpists have figured out that, in a post-natural world, the fact of being on one planet, sharing one atmosphere, does not mean we are in this together. Catastrophe will be manageable enough for the wealthy that it will not really feel like catastrophe, anyway not for a while. The world in 2100 may well be no more dangerous for them than the world of middle-class Americans in 1950 or that of Gilded Age plutocrats in 1890. In any case, imagining that they will be fine, and so will most of their grandchildren, is enough for them. At the least, for them this bet seems better than the risk of opening up economic life and global order to the challenges that would come from an honest confrontation with climate change. As long as enough voters identify with this willed complacency, it will be true, for all relevant purposes, that you can build a wall high enough to keep out climate change.

Thoreau insisted that democratic community is utterly real, as real as dirt, because we are trapped in it, because the facts we majoritarian bandits choose become the facts we live with every day. Politics is how a moral lie becomes a physical truth. After you lose a country you continue to wake up in it every morning. This has never been more true than today, when the emissions we ignore come back in the weather and the poisons we would rather not see follow us everywhere in the water and soil.

Thoreau's conclusion in "Slavery in Massachusetts" was a hopeful one: he came across a water lily in the swamp, and took its sweet smell as a symbol of a higher moral possibility. It was untainted by compromise with slavery, he said, and had never heard of politics. But today all of our lilies have heard of climate change. Their very bodies are different in a world with more carbon in the air and more heat in the long summers. There is no total refuge in the swamp flowers.

Here I leave Thoreau because he no longer seems the best guide to the value of his own thought. Thoreau's nature, at his most radical moments, is not a simple comfort, and also not a mirror, let alone an escape into beauty amid the mud. His nature tugs and jostles him to new vantage points. He looked to mountains because "their mere distance" was a kind of encouragement: an opened view in space could open the mind. He let his mind float down a stream and thought it was like seeing the earth from a distance, coming unmoored from the thudding impact that reminds you with every step of just where you are. In *Walden*, he wrote, "We are not wholly involved in Nature: I may be either the driftwood in the stream, or Indra in the sky looking down on it." This nature is part of one technique for opening a compressed and desperate mind that the world's events are occupying like a hostile force. The Thoreau I come to feels the accumulated violence of the country in his body. This is the Thoreau who wrote, defending John Brown's antislavery insurrection, "We preserve the so-called peace of our country by deeds of petty violence every day. Look at the policeman.... Look at the jail! Look at the gallows! We are hoping only to live safely on the outskirts of this provisional army." He denounced anyone who hoped to see change come from "quiet diffusion of the sentiments of humanity," answering, "As if the sentiments of humanity were ever found unaccompanied by deeds."

He laid claim to citizenship, not just as a privilege to be confessed, not just as an ideological trick to be unmasked, but as his biggest problem, something utterly real from which he could not separate himself, and for which he was owed no redress—a landscape that he needed to find complex ways to inhabit, understand, and try to change from within.

4

THE WORLD WE HAVE BUILT

Hurricane Florence dropped thirty-five inches of rain onto eastern North Carolina in September 2018, killing 41 people in the state, along with 5500 hogs and more than three million chickens and turkeys. Floodwater cut off the coastal city of Wilmington by road, while the Neuse River menaced Goldsboro, home of the Reverend William Barber's congregation, and the Cape Fear River swamped Fayetteville, near the Army's Fort Bragg. In my neighborhood in Durham, 140 miles inland, we perched safely but uneasily on the edge of catastrophe. Anything outside was damp. Anything mobile was ruffled by breezes. Warm humidity streaked condensed water across the windows of air-conditioned houses, and people stayed indoors refreshing weather updates.

If anything, Durham overprepared. Schools and city offices closed. Universities urged students to evacuate the region. Big-box stores were stripped of water, batteries, and other emergency supplies, and gas stations were empty. At home, we stockpiled jugs of water, dried fruit and canned beans, candles.

Disaster planning requires an accounting of everyday dependencies. How far can we drive if there is no gas for sale? Can we get to someplace where we know people? Without electricity, how many hours of light do we have? If the stores aren't restocked, when will we run out of food? How many phone numbers do we actually know by memory? How many people do we know who live in walking distance? As we pulled the counterfactual plug on one vital system after another, tasks that seemed straightforward—making a cup of coffee or washing clothes—became lost arts, minor superpowers, unsung miracles.

A recent study by geologist Jan Zalasiewicz and twenty-four coauthors estimated the total weight of human infrastructure—buildings, roads, vehicles, intensely cultivated cropland—at thirty trillion tons, roughly four thousand tons for every human being. In 2013, Peter Haff, a Duke University earth scientist, reckoned that without this infrastructure, which he calls "the technosphere," the human population "would quickly decline toward its Stone Age base of no more than ten million." You can relax that pessimism by an order of magnitude and still conclude that most of us would not survive outside our artificial habitat. We would be what Shakespeare's King Lear calls "unaccommodated man": a "poor, bare, forked animal" not equipped to last.

A "natural disaster," then, is at least half unnatural, the product of a natural event and the infrastructure that it floods, shakes, or ignites. In North Carolina, much of that infrastructure is agricultural: over the past thirty years, the eastern part of the state has become the slaughterhouse of the East Coast. At least six million pigs live here, mostly in "confined animal feeding operations" that contain thousands of animals apiece. Operators cure pig feces in open-air "lagoons" near the crowded barns where the animals spend their short lives. Poultry farms, which use the same model, are also widespread. In September 1999, Hurricane Floyd's floodwaters drowned a million chickens and turkeys and a hundred thousand hogs in eastern North Carolina, and sent 120 million gallons of their waste into the region's rivers. State officials marshaled incinerators to burn the corpses, and contamination persisted in waterways until the spring.

After that catastrophe, the hog industry got more careful about where it located facilities, and state lawmakers toughened environmental standards for new operations. But climate change has increased the vulnerability of North Carolina's low-lying eastern plain, expanding the size and water mass of hurricanes by as much as 50 percent, with ocean levels creeping up. Meanwhile, a Republican-dominated state legislature cut taxes and took other measures that blocked the development of a more resilient infrastructure. A 2012 statute initially forbade state planners from taking climate change into account, out of fear of burdening developers in storm-prone areas; the legislature softened it only when the Republican governor's office made clear that it would not make life harder for coastal builders.

In the event, Florence killed many fewer animals than Floyd had, but it flooded or came close to flooding roughly one hundred of the four thousand waste lagoons that North Carolina's more than twenty-two hundred hog farms maintain. Just two lagoons in Duplin and Sampson counties, which sit south of Goldsboro and inland of Wilmington, spilled more than seven million gallons of contaminated water into the South River and the Northeast Cape Fear River. The contamination that remained when the flood receded fell unequally on North Carolinians. It always does. Poor, rural, disproportionately nonwhite people live near the hog farms, which take root where land is cheap and political opposition is weak. They tend to live on flood-prone land and to rely on easily contaminated wells for their drinking water. The pork industry is rich and politically influential, and in the past two years the state legislature has changed state law to protect hog operations from suits by neighbors whose health and property are damaged by pollution. None of this is new. The modern environmental justice movement was born in Afton, North Carolina, in a fight over the state's decision to dump contaminated soil near a poor, historically African American community. Wilmington and other down-east towns carry the burdens of

Superfund sites and coal-ash ponds, which hold the toxic by-products of coal-fired electricity.

As usual, many people were extraordinarily good to one another. In Durham, during the long period of waiting and a spate of flash foods as the storm left the region headed north toward the Appalachian Mountains, neighbors checked in on one another, young people showed up to stay with the elderly, and trays of cookies and empanadas went from door to door. Down east, volunteers reached flooded houses in their personal boats, pulling people out of danger. When the roads were clear, we bought a carload of diapers, batteries, and bottled water and loaded it onto a flatbed truck headed for Goldsboro, helped by the mix of gray-haired Quakers and charismatic punks (who may also have been Quakers) that we had learned to experience as quintessential civic Durham. But what gets rebuilt will remain dangerously vulnerable to a warming world and will continue to share out its dangers unequally.

When a double rainbow appeared over Durham's gentrified downtown the evening after the storm had passed, the biblical sign of the Covenant seemed premature with the Neuse and Cape Fear rivers still surging toward their peaks. It also seemed archaic, a promise that Creation would always be a secure human home, a reassurance dating from a time before human beings became the creators of their own world. Between 1950 and 2015, nitrogen synthesized for fertilizers rose from less than four million tons annually to more than eighty-five million, and plastics production increased in weight from under one million tons to over three hundred million. The thirty trillion tons of global technosphere is some five orders of magnitude greater than the weight of the human beings that it sustains. And in the midst of all that, embraced by my four-thousand-ton share (more or less) of technosphere and hatching contingency plans for a world without clean water, communications, fuel, electricity, or a source of food, I was enacting an inadvertent meditation on human nature in the twenty-first century. "Unaccommodated man," to borrow Shakespeare's phrase again, is like an oyster ripped from its shell. For the most of us, a collective technological exoskeleton, circulatory system, and network of nerves form the conditions of our existence. Apart from them, we would have no being that would last long. We are creatures of our built environment, an infrastructure species.

Our species' infrastructure is the technosphere of roads, rails, utility lines, farmland, and housing. It also has a broader sense, in which it encompasses all the artificial systems that enable people to survive together and to reach one another for communication and cooperation. These include immaterial systems that connect people, such as money and the law of contracts that binds economic relationships. Although this second type of infrastructure may be immaterial, its effects are very material: it shapes the world's economies, and these in turn shape the global carbon cycle, the food system, mineral extraction (global steel production in this century alone has risen from 400 million annual tons to 1,150 million tons, driven mostly by China's vast growth), and so forth. The third kind of infrastructure follows directly from the second. It comprises the basic domains and cycles of the natural world: the global atmosphere, the water cycles and waterways, the soil and its fertility. The health of these has always sustained human power and thriving. They are the first great objects of human dependence: our reliance on them is the model for understanding our reliance today on roads and cables. It makes sense to call these systems infrastructure because they are increasingly what human beings have made, from the chemistry of the atmosphere and the microbiology of the soil to the ways water flows across the continents.

What does it mean to call humanity an infrastructure species? Think just once more of Lear's "unaccommodated man." There is scarcely such a thing as a human being apart from our shared and artificial world: concrete and cable and energy flows; legal regimes for coordinating activity, from property and contract law to the European Union's Common Fisheries Policy; and orders of power and authority, including ways of changing the other systems through political decisions and state power. It is within this complex housing that we answer the question "What shall we do today?" which, answered many times over, generates responses to the questions "Who are we?" and "What sort of world is this?" The human species is remaking the planet as an integrated piece of global infrastructure—in its artificial carbon and nitrogen cycles, climatic patterns, energy flows, biodiversity, and skin of roads, farmland, and settlements.

None of this is meant as a celebration of triumphant human control over the natural world. It is,

instead, a try at naming a problem that has us all—
however unequally—in its grip, one that human
beings have made but have no clear way to master.
One way to put the problem is this. A world that is
pervasively human-made presents a question: "What
sort of world shall we make?" One way or another,
that question is going to get answered. It gets answered every day, with every tank of gas, every new
ton of steel forged or concrete poured, every new
North Carolina hog farm with a farmer who owns
the waste lagoon, neighbors who deal with the contamination, Smithfield Foods owning the hogs that
the farmers raise on contract, and Chinese corporate
owners headquartered in Luohe, Henan province,
who ultimately control Smithfield's global holdings
of hog farms, slaughterhouses, and processing plants.
But in these trillions of world-making choices (many
thousands apiece every year by billions of people), it
is no one's job to see the whole, any more than it was
the job of Freedom Industries' CEO to think of the
health of the Elk River and the security of families
in Charleston, West Virginia, where the Elk joins
the Great Kanawha.

And it's worse than that. The problem is not simply purblindness, helter-skelter pursuit of preferences

without a bigger picture. The world we make tells us how to live in it, makes us know our place. The roads and flight routes, data networks and power grids are not optional. They are the only ways for most of us to serve our need to stay warm in the winter, keep the temperature at sleeping levels in the summer, eat enough to survive—let alone exercise our human powers to communicate with others, work and play, and feel ourselves part of the cultures in which we share. Our exoskeleton is also the groove in which we make our world-making choices. Global markets for capital and goods set the world's resources, from rare earths and soil fertility to the atmosphere's carbon-absorbing power, in a potentially universal cash nexus. The fate of the earth's resources is already sketched in the future of supply and demand, written in the markets as if in the stars. Although technological innovation can change cost structures, the larger logic of directing resources toward those who can pay for and profit from them is as comprehensive and unrelenting as a Stalinist five-year plan. The increasingly global market, which is also increasingly a market in everything, is one of the most fateful aspects of planetary infrastructure.

Our behavior, from individual choice through the decisions of corporations that are bigger than some countries, puts a crushing strain on planetary systems. For this reason, to go on living together we need to change the ways we shape the earth, bend them in the direction of a nondestructive and equitable commonwealth, or federation of commonwealths. But the institutions we have built fail to achieve this. This failure is their defining characteristic in the age of ecological crisis. The failure of our institutions is not happenstance, but occurs for reasons well canvassed in the literature of collective action: our choices are self-interested, short term, and, at their largest effective scale, national, while our problems are interdependent, long term, and global. Our infrastructures of choice—markets and governments—systemically lead us away from the most important problems. So we live within institutions and practices that have been refuted by circumstances, shown to be inadequate, but nevertheless persist. They work as a kind of fate, which humans made, which now makes us. We have made something unremitting in its command over its inhabitants, but in a deep way unchosen.

So it is urgent to ask: What human powers can help to change this world, make it something chosen and common? The weight of our made world—its technological infrastructure and its markets—may account for the kind of transformative action that is often easiest to imagine today: the hack. The hack is for the technosphere what the prayer of an adept once was for seeking divine intervention: a way of getting inside the mind of the ultimate sovereign. The hack is a way of pursuing system-level agency in the absence of political capacity to act at the scale of the system. Seen in this way, it is a new expression of one of the oldest forms of action: murmuring just the formula that will move the mind and hand of a ruler that is not accountable but might be susceptible to an aptly phrased appeal. The apt chemical or software or other engineering formula really can flow into the infrastructure of Leviathan's circuitry and make it cleaner, faster, cheaper—change, in other words, its dictates to us and make this infrastructure species over into a different species, one less impersonally devoted to ravaging the planet in order to live. Such a hack promises today to do what Rousseau said a lawgiver must be prepared to do: to change the nature of human beings by changing the world that orchestrates our choices, actions, and lives.

But hoping to be saved by a hack is like adopting the mind-set of Homeric protagonists, anxious for some capricious god to tweak the rules on their behalf. It is not a way of facing one another, a form of collective power over our own direction, or an ambition to count every voice equally. In this moment of elite pessimism about democracy, ecological disaster can seem one more reason to suppose that we cannot save ourselves—only a god of tech can save us. Putting hope in the hack gives up on specifically political, let alone democratic, responses to environmental questions. This is in contrast to the moment, now almost fifty years ago, when U.S. lawmakers passed national laws in response to the pollution and extinction crises that had arisen from the post–Second World War acceleration of human impact on the planet. The public and legislative discourse around those crises combined apocalyptic warnings with supreme confidence in the capacity of the institutions that had to avert apocalypse. The world might be ending, if we did nothing; but we had the power to do what needed doing.

That, anyway, was the story that got told again and again in those years. The beginning of modern environmental lawmaking was the last domestic act of the New Deal state (which was also of course the Cold War state and, accordingly, the state of U.S. hegemony over much of the world). Legislators assumed that they could retool national capitalism. The activist and radical wings of organized labor talked about striking to enforce environmental and health and safety standards. Most of that would seem fantastical today. But maybe it need not.

■ ■ ■

If humanity has become an infrastructure species, we also remain what Aristotle long ago described us as being: *zoon politikon*, the political animal. As a political species, we have the power to choose the shape of our shared existence. The principles, practices, and institutions that we create through this power are just as artificial, and potentially just as important, as the more literally weighty technosphere. Consider some words whose meaningfulness and power we take for granted: *rights*, *citizen*, *vote*, *democracy*, *legitimacy*. These are not *things* in the way that a chair or a stone is a thing. You can't kick a vote. You can't measure it in the most sophisticated physics lab. But you can steal it, as you can violate a right even though you cannot point to it. Such things as rights and votes are real because, like a goal in soccer, they name part of a practice whose meaning and consequences its members understand as they understand up and down or light and dark—as parts of the framework of the world. These artificial realities change who we are to one another and what we are capable of doing: citizen of a democracy, person disenfranchised by a felony conviction, refugee with asylum rights, stateless person.

The great power of a political species is to change the architecture of its common world. Consider, for example, the creation of a constitution, the establishment of universal suffrage, the abolition of enslaved labor, the assertion of public control over key institutions such as roads, railways, hospitals, or banks. Or consider the environmental laws that came into force in the 1970s to afford new protections to the nonhuman world and place new obligations on property owners and businesses. Such a change makes a new world, sometimes in modest ways, sometimes sweepingly. This power of world making is doubly important to a political species that is also an infrastructure species. In making our political world, we also decide, explicitly or implicitly, how to shape the half-artificial planet that is our home in the Anthropocene. This means that political change is the one way to work an intentional transformation in the built world. That world, as we have seen, tells us how to live in it, and more specifically determines the environmental damage that we do simply by participating in social life. By changing it, we change ourselves—change what we are to one another and to the planet.

Political decisions answer questions such as: Will roads, rails, or bicycle paths be built here? Will coal be mined, or solar panels erected? If we answer these questions through markets, what are the rules that define the markets? How much does carbon cost? Do prices reflect the marginal convenience of current buyers and sellers, or are they an attempt to value the whole living world and future generations? Will we rebuild the national economy, and help to redirect the world economy, in a green and just shape—what some of us call a Green New Deal? Taken together, the answers to these questions make a world. For an infrastructure species, political sovereignty can transform world making—which is also collective self making—into a deliberate act.

This uniquely constructive power of political sovereignty is especially worth insisting on at a time when some of the world's most powerful states form an Axis of Denial, in which refusing to seriously acknowledge or do anything about climate change is a point of convergence for constituencies from the coal industry to the religious right. Climate denial is also a kind of ecological symbol of a broader denial: denial that U.S. demographics are changing, that the revolution in gender roles and identity is here to stay and should keep unfolding, that the racial history of the United States is still mainly without reparation. Border walls have become the emblem of this use of sovereignty to secure the fragmentation of the planet into gated communities and sacrifice zones. Sovereignty in these uses works to create, ratify, and extend unequal and exploitative relations. Humanity has achieved its inequality. But the state, the weaponized tool of the worst things we do—against one another and the rest of life—is also the way to a different situation.

Today the power to decide which infrastructure to make—which means, in a real way, choosing what sort of species we are going to be—often feels like more of a pious wish than a potent reality. Consider a comment in the journal *Bioscience* that appeared in 2017, a sequel to a 1992 document called the "World Scientists' Warning to Humanity." Both the 1992 piece and the 2017 article are built around a kind of graphic that readers will know well: trend lines for key environmental indicators such as available fresh water per capita (down), populations of wild vertebrates (down), carbon dioxide emissions (up), deforestation (up), and oxygen-starved "dead zones" in bodies of water that receive large doses of agricultural runoff (up). The graphs portray a planet moving deeper into mass extinction, strain or exhaustion of life-giving resources like water, and massive climate change. The 1992 version of the warning had more than 1700 scientist signatories, including more than half the living Nobel laureates in the sciences. The 2017 version had more than fifteen thousand scientist signatories from 184 countries—a rate of growth that resembles its other trend lines.

The scientists' warning is addressed to "humanity," and the text includes the declaration that "humanity must practice a more environmentally sustainable alternative" as well as a list of "steps humanity can take to transition to sustainability." On one level, the phrases name a bare fact. If these changes do not happen, we know, roughly, what the result will be, even if many of us have trouble really fathoming how bad it will be. Familiar formulas still spring to the lips, or to the tweeting fingertips: If not now, when? We are all in this together!

On another level, the "humanity" that the self-described "world scientists" address does not exist. There is no "we" that could take the actions that the scientists call for. Collective decisions, world-shaping decisions, come through political institutions with the power to issue and enforce regimes of cooperation—legal infrastructure—and those political institutions do not exist. The "humanity" that the scientists appeal to floats insubstantially above actual political choices.

The appeal to humanity is at once cogent and nonsensical, urgent and pointless. The heavy facts of a fragmented and unequal world contradict the scientists' call at every point, but they don't disestablish it. Here is our paradox: the world can't go on this way; and it can't do otherwise. It was the collective power of some—not all—human beings that got us into this: power over resources, power over the seasons, power over one another. That power has created a global humanity, entangled in a Frankenstein ecology. But it does not yet include the power of accountability or restraint, the power we need. To face the Anthropocene, humans would need a way of facing one another. We would need, first, to be a we.

There is a well-established way of arguing about sovereignty that goes back to Thomas Hobbes's *Leviathan*. Show what problems a sovereign— meaning the collective decision making of a political community—must be able to solve. If you show that the existing form or theory of sovereignty can't address that problem successfully, then you've shown its inadequacy. In a certain way you've refuted it. Hobbes famously argued in this way that the problem of order among human beings was too deep-seated and persistent to be resolved by any regime that lacked certain kinds of scope and decisiveness: with weak, uncertain, or divided sovereignty, the sources of conflict that political institutions were meant to tame would instead colonize politics, producing irresolvable conflict. The force of Hobbes's argument was that basic forms of order and the security they bring are preconditions of any tolerable social life. A putative sovereign that can't secure such order has no claim on obedience. We have made a world that cannot go on, but goes on, stumbling, it seems, toward catastrophe. What can, what might, we do?

It often strikes people that a global problem requires a global government, and they either press toward that faraway horizon or recoil from it—a reaction that can motivate climate denial and other rejections of interdependence. But although it is true that interdependence brings moral responsibilities, it is not true that a global state must arise to meet global crises. This is good news because the crises are running well ahead of any prospect of a global state. It matters less what the scale of a political community is than whether it succeeds in being a commonwealth. If it does—if it aims successfully at making a free community of equals in a nondestructive economy—then it will stand a good chance of helping to form an international community of commonwealths. A global commonwealth need not be a single state. It needs only to be a community oriented to commonwealth ideals.

What do those principles mean when taken to the global scale? They mean that distributional questions,

questions of global justice, are inevitable. Ecological and other planetary systems impose limits on the lives they can sustain among billions of people. The market-first solution to these questions is to suppress them in favor of an implicit assumption that an economic tide rising eventually reaches and lifts all boats. Joint decisions about priorities and needs get handed over to rising prices in an unequal world—which is just a way of making the same decisions sub silentio and calling their inequities "efficient." But in the age of climate change the image of rising tides suggests selective catastrophe, not universal bounty. A commonwealth in a community of commonwealths must take seriously the obligation to share a finite world—to share its good things and to share in the burdens of repairing it and keeping it whole, including the burden of using our political power to adopt limits on what we demand of the planet.

The world belongs in principle to all who are born into it. It is morally arbitrary that we open our eyes in a world already parceled out and owned. This is a difficult thought to put to work, but it is a necessary egalitarian starting point. The world's inequalities, however written they are into its many material and legal infrastructures, must be seen as subject to judgment and revision. A commonwealth's engagement with the problem of global sharing must start from the premise that everyone alive has an equal claim to thrive in this world. A commonwealth must not deny care, a share, to others simply because they are other. A commonwealth among commonwealths may encompass debate between those who push toward open borders and those who prefer aid, fair trade, and reparations for a history of international violence and destruction. But two other poles are anathema to the commonwealth ideal: first, the nationalist principle of building solidarity (usually an unequal and internally hierarchical form, but in any case) on the denial that anyone but our compatriots can have any claim on us; and second, the market-first form of global integration that extends the extractive, inequality-producing logic of commodification and "return on investment" across the planet. One turns inward, the other outward, but neither takes seriously the principles of human equality and ecological care at the heart of commonwealth.

We need sovereignty, national and international, to do this work. But the sovereigns we have are often grotesque impresarios of denialism, like the American president. People of conscience end up being, de facto, against sovereignty, because they encounter it mainly as a vehicle of this kind of politics—and why would you not oppose that? Seeing the state as a site of adequate responses to the present has, ironically, the cast of utopianism right now.

So we need, at least, to be able to name an agent of politics that could orient itself toward these territorial states with the right kind of demands. But what is that agent? The left has been looking for it since the failure of working-class internationalism to emerge as a democratic and revolutionary force. The neoliberals have the market-making state, the corporation, and the perennial rearrangement of human relations under the joint sway of these (which they may like to call spontaneous order); and they have the figure of the entrepreneur. The neoconservatives have the militaries. The new populists of the right have the resentments and enthusiasms of nationalism—now, in many countries, at the reins of the market-making state. None of these really tries to grapple with our tyrannical global infrastructure Leviathan. All can be read as, in some way, symptoms of it. The left risks being merely symptomatic too, the chattering conscience of this world.

We need an internationalism that works through national sovereignties because our problems are global and our power to change the rules collectively is mostly national. We need an internationalism that raises questions of distribution and justice within the limits of an ultimately finite planet. We need deeper forms of security and solidarity because those are the beginnings of possibility for a politics that doesn't aim always at growth. We need these things to arise within relentless markets and in the face of selfish nationalism. It seems only fair to say that all of this might not be possible. It can only help, nonetheless, to know and not let one another forget that it is what we need.

5

THE LONG ENVIRONMENTAL JUSTICE MOVEMENT

As I write, one of the most popular and polarizing politicians in the country is Representative Alexandria Ocasio-Cortez of New York. She has drawn energy to the Green New Deal, a vision of environmentalism as a program for justice and care in both economy and ecology. She decided to run for Congress after visiting Standing Rock, in the Dakotas, to join Sioux protestors and environmentalist supporters in opposing the Dakota Access Pipeline. That action, which convinced the Obama administration not to approve the pipeline (before the Trump administration changed course and restarted the project), was an unusual piece of radical, sustained resistance in an environmental movement that has recently prized its establishment access and reputation for technocratic sobriety. But Bernie Sanders, whose presidential campaign Ocasio-Cortez had joined as an organizer, called for "keeping it in the ground"— ending dependence on fossil fuels and pressing for a fast transition to renewable energy. The Movement for Black Lives had called for divestment from fossil fuels. An insurrection was growing that saw the fossil fuel industry, along with the vast infrastructure of pipelines, refineries, and highways that made it seem so cost-efficient and "natural," as a kind of hostile occupying force, weighing heavily on the planet and on the ethical and ecological possibilities of our lives. Confrontations between fossil fuel power and indigenous peoples such as the Standing Rock Sioux made especially vivid what it means to call our energy economy "extractive": it took land from those who first lived there, as it takes energy from the ground, and in both cases the taking is unreciprocated. By virtue of living in this energy economy, we are all in debt, historically and ecologically, to those who have carried the burdens and to the natural world that we keep breaking beyond its power to heal itself. To go on in this way is, as Thoreau realized when he lost his country, not innocent but closer to criminal. We have lost not just a country but a world—that is, the possibility of believing in the innocence of the world we have built, a world we cannot escape but can only take responsibility for and try to redeem. The question is how to redeem it, how to take it back.

This is the affirmative vision that follows and completes the rejection of fossil fuels. Ocasio-Cortez calls herself a democratic socialist. What she seems to mean by the name is that we have in common the things we choose to share together, and these common things—good schools, good transport, public parks, good housing, and medical care for everyone—make a shared world. We should make them everyone's. The name is also a way of claiming a long tradition of politics that asks not whether the world is good enough or getting better, but instead what is the gap between the world we have now and the better world that is within our power to make. It is a tradition that recognizes that economies do not just produce wealth: they produce human lives and relationships, which can be dignified or humiliating, mutual or exploitative, solidaristic or fragmenting, more frightening or safer. And economies, in turn, do not arise naturally, whether from the self-interest of "rational man" or from the disruptive imagination of entrepreneurs and the benignity of philanthropists. Political decisions give economies their shape, from labor laws and tax rates and public investments to questions of almost metaphysical significance. The journalist Kate Aronoff has observed that climate politics addresses the question of who will survive the twenty-first century. Environmental politics, like the politics of work and health care, answers in very concrete terms the ultimate question: What is the value of life? And whose life, which lives, will be valued? As I write, a hopeful, even heroic response to these questions is gathering under the heading of the Green New Deal. Maybe it will find another banner soon, or maybe it will succeed in transforming the meaning of the New Deal from the industrial, racially exclusionary, male-centered program of solidarity that it was to a truly universal reworking of its potential into a commonwealth of shared dignity and mutual care.

I don't mean to make too much hang on the person of Alexandria Ocasio-Cortez or the slogan she has helped to elevate. Like the Sanders campaign that shaped her political work, she has become prominent in part because of charisma and courage, but more because the moment needs her. Movements, organizing work, teaching and learning, suffering and reflection, all come together from many places in the power of any political leader. But what the leader shows back matters too, helps the rest of us to give voice to what we are trying to do, to understand our own responsibilities and desires.

The transformation that some call a Green New Deal, the move to commonwealth politics, would not just radicalize economic policy. It would radicalize environmentalism—in the double sense of transforming it and returning it to its roots. Joining environmentalism to movements for deep economic and racial justice wouldn't be new. It would shift the movement toward what you might think of as its left wing, often called the environmental justice movement, which emerged in the 1980s as an internal criticism of "mainstream environmentalism" for being too elite, too white, and too focused on beautiful scenery and charismatic species. It would also point toward a longer history, now mostly forgotten. For decades, environmentalism and what we now call environmental justice were deeply intertwined. Care for the earth and for vulnerable human communities belonged together. Empowering workers, protecting public health, and preserving landscapes were parts of a single effort. Spurred by the moment of the Green New Deal, it is time to reclaim that older environmental movement and see that it was an environmental justice movement all along.

Modern environmental law is defined by a set of statutes that were adopted in a burst of legislation in the 1970s: the National Environmental Policy Act on New Year's Day, 1970; the Clean Air Act later in 1970; the Clean Water Act in 1972; the Endangered Species Act in 1973; laws governing waste disposal and reworking the management of federal public lands in 1976. Environmentalism is also defined by a set of advocacy organizations that grew up in the same years: the Natural Resources Defense Council (NRDC), the Environmental Defense Fund, the Sierra Club Legal Defense Club (which later became Earthjustice, a major environmental litigation group), and the Environmental Law Institute all either appeared or took their current form in these years. The advocacy groups are an important part of the story because they help to define the field. Environmental law has always been susceptible to identity crisis. It doesn't have the unifying textual basis of constitutional law, the doctrinal coherence of tort or contract, or the straightforward topical boundaries of antitrust or tax law. Instead, it has an organizing principle that might be thought of as "everything is connected." What counts as environmentalism has always been partly a matter of the priorities of movements and advocates.

Environmental justice scholars and advocates have made three especially important criticisms of mainstream environmentalism. First, it doesn't speak enough to how environmental harms and benefits are distributed, which is urgent when distribution follows the lines of poverty and race. This criticism arises from the grassroots fights that produced the modern environmental justice movement: fights about decisions to place garbage dumps, toxic waste sites, incinerators, and power plants in neighborhoods where disproportionately poor and nonwhite people lived. The environmental statutes of the 1970s accomplished many things, but they did not prohibit these disproportionate impacts. Second, environmental justice critics challenge the mainstream idea of what environmental problems are in the first place. They say it's focused on the beautiful outdoors, has an antiurban bias, and isn't engaged enough with artificial human environments like neighborhoods and workplaces. As one pair of pioneering environmental justice scholar-activists wrote, the environments we most care about should be "the places where we live, work, learn, and play," whether they are natural or built. And while more prosperous people tend to take clean and safe living spaces for granted and to be able to escape to wild places that feel "ecological" or "natural," poor people often have very little choice but to spend their lives in compromised artificial environments. Third, mainstream environmentalism overvalues elite forms of advocacy, like litigation and high-level lobbying, and doesn't make enough room for popular engagement. It creates a movement of professionals and experts: lawyers, economists, and ecologists who have limited interaction with, and do too little to empower, the people who live with the most severe environmental problems.

■ ■ ■

And it gets worse. Deeper in its history, environmental politics has not just failed to combine human and ecological caretaking, justice to people and right use of land. It has sometimes pitted them against each other, powering conservation with the aversive energy of racism and misanthropy. In this respect, the history of environmentalism is a microcosm of American history generally. From the solidarity and caretaking of a New Deal that was also patriarchal and racist to the history of a constitutional democracy that has been both egalitarian and hierarchical, this country's inheritance is essentially divided within and against itself. Aziz Rana calls this deep fact the "two faces of American freedom." From the beginning, the country was built on a more radical respect for the equal freedom of its insiders—white male citizens—than any other in the world. At the same time, it was among the cruelest in its domination and exploitation of "outsiders," especially enslaved and indigenous people, women, and those who did not fit its gender and sexual norms. The challenge for American radicals has always been to cut this knot by building a world in which everyone is an insider, a world without caste, exploitation, or social cruelty. The American temptation and betrayal has always been to break movements toward commonwealth on the stone of the bigotry and fear of today's insiders, deepening divisions and keeping the world unkind and unsafe. After Emancipation, radical Reconstruction moved toward a nation of equal citizenship, and racial reaction broke it. The New Deal and the Great Society built an American conception of economic citizenship, of material security and dignity alongside legal rights. Racism and sexism confined, eroded, and ultimately undercut these gains, and a divided United States became more unequal and insecure than European countries that, 120 years ago, were far more deeply torn between rich and poor than the young United States. Hamstringing itself with fear of real solidarity, the American majority changed places with Europe and built a new Gilded Age of rich and poor.

The same history has riven environmentalism, compromising and even poisoning its promise of commonwealth. Take Madison Grant (Yale College 1887, Columbia Law School), who was instrumental in creating the Bronx Zoo and founded the first organizations dedicated to preserving American bison and the California redwoods. He belonged, like his political ally Teddy Roosevelt, to a Manhattan aristocracy defined by bloodline and money and spent his career at the center of the same conservationist circle as Roosevelt. This band of reformers did much to create the country's national parks, for-ests, game refuges, and other public lands—the system of environmental stewardship and public use that has been called "America's best idea." They developed the conviction that a country's treatment of its land and wildlife is a measure of its character. And Grant could be prescient: In an industrial era when humanity had achieved "complete mastery of the globe," Grant wrote in 1909, his generation had "the responsibility of saying what forms of life shall be preserved."

Few environmentalists remember Madison Grant. He has been pushed to the margins of movement history for the same reason that he is sometimes remembered in other circles: his 1916 book *The Passing of the Great Race, or The Racial Basis of Euro-pean History*, a pseudoscientific work of white su-premacism that warns of the decline of the "Nordic" peoples. In Grant's racial theory, Nordics were a natu-ral aristocracy, marked by noble, generous instincts and a gift for political self-governance, who were being overtaken by the "Alpine" and "Mediterranean" populations. Grant's work influenced the racist Im-migration Act of 1924, which restricted migration from Eastern and Southern Europe and Africa and banned migrants from the Middle East and Asia. Adolf Hitler wrote Grant an admiring letter, calling the book "my Bible," which has given it permanent status on the far right. Anders Breivik, the Norwegian extremist who killed sixty-nine young Labour Party members in 2011, drew on Grant's racial theory in his own horrible manifesto against immigration to twenty-first-century Europe.

Grant's fellow conservationists supported his racist activism. Roosevelt wrote Grant a letter praising *The Passing of the Great Race* that appeared as a blurb on later editions, calling it "a capital book; in purpose, in vision, in grasp of the facts our people most need to realize." Henry Fairfield Osborn, who headed the New York Zoological Society and the board of trustees of the American Museum of Natural History (and, as a member of the U.S. Geological Survey, named the *Tyrannosaurus rex* and the *Velociraptor*), wrote a foreword to the book. Osborn argued that "conservation of that race which has given us the true spirit of Americanism is not a matter either of racial pride or of racial prejudice; it is a matter of love of country." This willful, disingenuous blending of racism with what is sometimes called "American nationalism" remains familiar today.

For Grant, Roosevelt, and other architects of the country's parks and game refuges, wild nature was worth saving for its aristocratic qualities; where these were lacking, the pioneering conservationists were indifferent. Grant, as his *Times* obituary noted, "was uninterested in the smaller forms of animal or bird life." He wrote about the moose, the mountain goat, and the redwood tree, whose nobility and need for protection in a venal world so resembled the plight of Grant's "Nordics" that his biographer, Jonathan Spiro, concludes that Grant as two faces of a single threatened aristocracy. Similarly, Roosevelt in his accounts of hunting could not say enough about the "lordly" and "noble" elk and buffalo that he and Grant helped to preserve and loved to kill. Their preservation work aimed to keep alive this kind of encounter between would-be aristocratic men and halfway wild nature. It was as much about preserving a modern version of England's royal game parks for the elites of industry and the professions as it was about the love of nature. More exactly, the nature they loved was the nature that made them feel noble, socially and, in their imaginations, racially.

For these conservationists, who prized the expert governance of resources as the supreme virtue of public policy, it was a short step from managing forests to managing the human gene pool. In a 1909 report to Roosevelt's National Conservation Commission, Yale professor Irving Fisher broke off from a discussion of public health to recommend preventing "paupers" and physically unhealthy people from reproducing and warned against the "race suicide" that would follow if the country did not replenish itself with Northern European stock. Fisher took the term "race suicide" from Roosevelt, who, in a 1905 speech, had pinned the crime on WASP women who dodged childbearing. Gifford Pinchot, the country's foremost theorizer and popularizer of conservation and head of Roosevelt's Forest Service, was a delegate to the first and second International Eugenics Congresses in 1912 and 1921 and a member of the advisory council of the American Eugenics Society from 1925 to 1935.

Roosevelt put Pinchot in charge of the National Conservation Commission, but he also cultivated the romantic naturalist John Muir, who founded the Sierra Club in 1892. In the Sierra Club's early leaders, the environmental movement has some less troubling ancestors than Grant and Roosevelt. Following Muir, whose bearded face and St. Francis–like persona were as much its icons as Yosemite Valley, the club adopted the gentle literary romanticism of Thoreau, Emerson, and Wordsworth. The point of preserving wild places, for these men—and, unlike in Roosevelt's circles, some women—was to escape the utilitarian grind of lowland life and, as Muir wrote, to see the face of God in the high country.

But Muir, who felt fraternity with four-legged "animal people" and even plants, was at best ambivalent about human brotherhood. Describing a thousand-mile walk from the Upper Midwest to the Gulf of Mexico, he reported the laziness of "Sambos." Later he lamented the "dirty and irregular life" of Indians in the Merced River valley near Yosemite. In "Our National Parks," a 1901 essay collection written to promote parks tourism, he assured readers that "as to Indians, most of them are dead or civilized into useless innocence." This might have been incisive irony, but in the same paragraph Muir was more concerned with human perfidy toward bears ("Poor fellows, they have been poisoned, trapped, and shot at until they have lost confidence in brother man") than with how Native Americans had been killed and driven from their homes.

It is easy to excuse such views as the "ordinary" or "casual" racism of the time, and Muir's comments do feel more like symptoms of the dominant culture than Grant's racism and Pinchot's eugenics, which touched the nerves of their basic commitments. But Muir and his followers were not ordinary representatives of their time. They are remembered because their respect for nonhuman life and wild places expanded the boundaries of moral concern for many who followed them. What does it mean that they cared more about "animal people" than about some human beings? The time they lived in is part of an explanation of what they wrote and felt, but not an excuse for today's environmentalists to shrug off the difficulty. For each of these environmentalist icons, the meaning of nature and wilderness was constrained, even produced, by an idea of civilization. Muir's nature was a pristine refuge from the city. Madison Grant's nature was the last redoubt of nobility in a leveling and hybridizing democracy. They went to the woods to escape aspects of humanity. They created and preserved versions of the wild that promised to exclude the human qualities they despised.

What became of all of this in the crucible of modern environmentalism, the mass movement and institution building of the 1970s, when the Sierra Club's membership grew from tens to hundreds of thousands and new groups arose: the NRDC, the Environmental Defense Fund, and many others? The older, exclusionary politics of nature had never gone away, and it ended up giving some of its shape to the new movement. In 1948, more than a decade before Rachel Carson's *Silent Spring*, a pair of best-selling works of popular ecology sounded many of Carson's themes, from the dangers of pesticides to the need to respect nature's harmonies. William Vogt's *Road to Survival* embraced eugenics as a response to overpopulation, urging governments to offer cash to the poor for sterilization, which would have "a favorable selective influence" on the species. In "Our Plundered Planet," Fairfield Osborn, the son of Madison Grant's friend and ally Henry Fairfield Osborn, forecast that postwar humanitarianism, which allowed ever more people to survive into adulthood, would prove incompatible with ecological limits. While neither man evinced Madison Grant's racial obsessions, they joined him in marshaling "nature" against a debased humanity that had grown past natural limits.

This strain of misanthropy appeared again in biologist Paul Ehrlich's 1968 runaway best seller *The Population Bomb*. Ehrlich illustrated overpopulation with a recollection of a Delhi slum seen through a taxi window: a "mob" with a "hellish aspect," full of "people eating, people washing, people sleeping.... People thrusting their hands through the taxi window, begging. People defecating.... People, people, people, people." He confessed to being afraid that he and his wife would never reach their hotel, and reported that on that night he came to understand overpopulation "emotionally." By the evidence, what he had encountered was not overpopulation but poverty. Ehrlich was announcing that his environmentalist imperatives were powered by fear and repugnance at slum dwellers leading their lives in public view. At the very least, he assumed that his readers would find his repugnance resonant, and he was glad to appeal to it.

Even as environmentalism took on big new problems in the 1970s, it also seemed to promise an escape hatch from continuing crises of inequality, social conflict, and, sometimes, certain kinds of people.

Time described the environmental crisis as a problem that Americans "might actually solve, unlike the immensely more elusive problems of race prejudice or the war in Vietnam." In his 1970 State of the Union address, in which he expended less than a hundred words on Vietnam, made no explicit reference to race, yet launched a new racialized politics with calls for a "war" on crime and attacks on the welfare system (the drift of his party's "Southern Strategy"), Richard Nixon spent almost a thousand words on the environment, which he called "a cause beyond party and beyond factions." That meant, of course, that he thought it could be a cause for the white majority he was working to assemble.

Environmentalism largely was just that in the seminal early 1970s. When the Sierra Club polled its members in 1972 on whether the club should "concern itself with the conservation problems of such special groups as the urban poor and ethnic minorities," 40 percent of respondents were strongly opposed and only 15 percent were supportive. Replies aside, the phrasing of the question made the club's premises clear enough. Admitting to its race problem took the movement nearly two decades. In 1987, the United Church of Christ's Commission for

Racial Justice published an influential report that found that hazardous waste facilities were disproportionately located in minority communities and called this unequal vulnerability "a form of racism." The environmental movement, the report observed, "has historically been white middle and upper-class." Three years later, activists sent a letter to the heads of major environmental organizations, reporting that nonwhites constituted less than 2 percent of the combined 745 employees of the Audubon Society, Sierra Club, NRDC, and Friends of the Earth. Fred Krupp, then executive director of the Environmental Defense Fund, replied with a mea culpa: "Environmental groups have done a miserable job of reaching out to minorities."

Since then, "environmental racism" and "environmental justice" have entered the vocabulary of the movement. There are many environmentalisms now, with their own constituencies and commitments. In the Appalachian coalfields, locals fight the mountaintop-removal strip mining that has shattered peaks and buried headwater streams. Activists from working-class Latino neighborhoods in Los Angeles opposed parts of California's landmark climate-change legislation, which the large environmental groups supported, arguing that it gave poor communities too little protection from concentrated pollution. Despite such conflicts, large, well-resourced national groups such the Sierra Club and the NRDC seek out these groups as partners in everything from environmental monitoring to lawsuits. Mitch Bernard, director of litigation at NRDC, says, "It's no longer a national group swooping down on a locale and saying this is what we think you should do. Much more of the impetus for action, and the strategies for action, come from the affected community." Still, because the major environmental statutes, such as the Clean Air Act and the Clean Water Act, do not create levers to address the unequal vulnerability of poor and minority groups, the priorities of the old environmental movement live on to limit effective legal strategies for activists today.

Some of the awkwardness of environmental politics since the 1970s, now even more acute in the age of climate change, is that it lays claim to worldwide problems, but brings to them some of the cultural habits of a more parochial and sometimes nastier movement. Ironically enough, Madison Grant, writing about extinction, was right: the natural world that future generations live in will be the one we create for them. Yet many of the environmentalist habits of thought that propose to inform this shaping of the future arose in an argument restricted to prosperous white people, some of them bigots and racial engineers, about the character and future of a country that they were sure was theirs and expected to keep.

■ ■ ■

But there is another history of environmentalism, a strand of efforts to build a political and economic community of common care. We do not need to be trapped by our history of self-division. When environmental justice activists and scholars take aim at what they call mainstream environmental law, they are addressing the statutes, agencies, and professional and advocacy organizations that were built in to their more or less current form in the 1970s and early 1980s. The environmental justice criticisms are essential, but the mainstream environmentalism whose narrowness they criticize was a recent development, one that might have turned out very differently. If we draw back the historical lens, a "long environmental justice movement" comes into view. In this movement, for more than a century, activists and scholars have been engaging the themes of fairness, inequality, and political and economic power in the human environment.

What was this movement? Here are some key examples. Two iconic environmental developments of the 1960s were the passage of the Wilderness Act in 1964 and (as mentioned a little earlier) the publication of Rachel Carson's *Silent Spring* between 1960 and 1962. The Wilderness Act has protected more than a hundred million acres of public land for hiking, camping, and solitude. It was a great victory for a long political drive to preserve public land that went back to the first national park, Yellowstone, designated in 1872. But its central value—wilderness, untouched land, set aside from all human contamination—seemed to prove that the movement that loved wild nature didn't care much about the places where people lived, worked, played, and learned. Environmental historian William Cronon made this point powerfully in 1995, when he argued that "the trouble with wilderness" was it that beckoned devotees to imagine that the only nature worth treasuring was pristine wildland, and encouraged them to ignore their own backyards.

Carson's *Silent Spring* described a poisoned world where pesticides passed through the air, water, and soil, to enter the flesh of animals and people, and spread sickness and death. The book helped to create a widespread ecological consciousness, and also to connect that consciousness with a sense of fear and crisis that helped to spur the 1970s antipollution statutes. But Carson's great elegy and polemic, which followed pesticides through almost their whole cycle of destruction, ignored the mainly Latino farm workers of California and Florida, who were directly exposed to pesticides in their work in the fields. The human victims of pesticides, in Carson's telling, lived in iconic small-town and suburban America. They were implicitly white and Anglo. They were not workers. So Carson, like the wilderness movement, can seem to prove that the narrowness as well as the power of mainstream environmentalism are there at the beginning.

But *Silent Spring* and the Wilderness Act were late chapters in earlier movements that made them possible. Those precursors were at the heart of the long environmental justice movement. The movement for wilderness was centered on the Wilderness Society, which was founded in 1935. A typical founder was Benton MacKaye, a planner and interdisciplinary intellectual who is also credited with the idea behind the Appalachian Trail. MacKaye defined "environment" as the built and industrial environment, just as much as the wild and natural one. His great example of ecological thinking was an image of New York City as composed of what he called "flows": the Hudson River and the Atlantic Ocean, the prevailing winds out of the west, but also barges of steel from the Great Lakes, ships full of grain steaming off to Europe, and the highways and railroads that drew workers into the city every morning and exhaled them again at night. He saw the struggles of factory workers and wilderness advocates as two parts of a movement with very large goals: to make the whole human environment, from the workplace to the untouched woods, welcoming and stimulating, a good place to be alive. He thought this required extensive and intensive public planning of cities, transport networks, and regions. For him, wilderness was one essential note in a larger composition of landscapes and living places.

Other wilderness activists stitched their environmentalism into similarly broad social concerns. MacKaye's cofounder and the president of the Wilderness Society was Robert Marshall, a forester who was also head of the Washington, D.C., branch of the American Civil Liberties Union, an avowed socialist, and a major figure in reforms that increased the sovereignty and cultural autonomy of Native American nations. Marshall's devotion to preserving wilderness was part of his broader vision of a just society. He believed that mental and spiritual freedom required the chance to escape to a place radically separate from everyday life, but there was nothing escapist in his politics. The wilderness movement that Marshall and MacKaye built was intensely concerned with the whole human environment, the condition of factory workers and people living in cities, and the role of the state in the economy and social life.

And what about Carson? The scholar whose earlier research runs all through *Silent Spring* is Wilhelm Hueper, an industrial toxicologist who devoted his career to understanding the effects of workplace exposure to what he called "the new artificial environment" of synthetic chemicals. His goal in understanding what the new poisons were doing to people was to secure "a healthful living, not merely for a small, select, and socially privileged class," but for everyone. He was working in a tradition of industrial toxicology that was pioneered a generation earlier by Alice Hamilton, the first woman faculty member at Harvard, a public health scholar who went into factories and worked with workers to understand what lead, phosphorous, and other chemicals were doing to their bodies. Also in the background of industrial toxicology were movements like the Workers' Health Bureau, a joint creation of women public health activists and independent unions, which researched workplace hazards, as its founders put it, "from the point of view of the worker." Carson's work was rooted in industrial toxicology, and that, in turn, was rooted in movements for social reform and efforts to build both workers' power and systems of industrial governance in the early twentieth century.

Why did these broader concerns not flower in the environmentalism that took shape in the burst of statutes and institution building in the 1970s? It is not that the architects of the modern environmental laws and institutions didn't care about these questions of equity and the total human environment. Rather, they thought they *were* addressing those questions. Senator Ed Muskie of Maine, a primary drafter of the antipollution statutes, explained at Earth Day 1970, "Man's environment includes more than natural resources. It includes the shape of the communities in which he lives: his home, his schools, his places of work." Muskie went on to argue that "the only kind of society that has a chance" is "a society that will not tolerate slums for some and decent houses for others, rats for some and playgrounds for others, clean air for some and filth for others." And he insisted that "those who believe that we are talking about the Grand Canyon and the Catskills, but not Harlem and Watts are wrong."

The environmental statutes were passed in a world where, from the point of view of their architects, they *were* environmental justice statutes. But that world was disappearing even as the new environmental laws were drafted. Those laws were written in a time that was more economically equal than the United States had ever been, or has been since, and their drafters believed that equality would continue and deepen, that economic inequality was a problem solved. We now know, thanks to the work of economist Thomas Piketty and others, that they were living at the end of an anomalous period of widely shared growth that lasted across the North Atlantic between the end of World War II and the beginning of the 1970s. Most periods of modern capitalism have seen growing inequality, not widely shared wealth. In the early 1970s inequality was about to reassert itself, and it has been growing more or less ever since.

Just as today's environmental justice critics say, the laws that govern pollution and disposal of hazardous materials don't address how those dangerous things get distributed. Leaving out distribution was a mistake that was much easier to make in good faith if you believed that the country was steadily getting more equal. The more recent environmental justice movement arose in response to the fact that environmental harms are distributed along very familiar lines of race and poverty. In the early 1970s, those lines were expected to become steadily less important. Legislators like Muskie also expected environmental laws to be bolstered by other reform legislation that would work to overcome poverty and social isolation, foster public health, and make workplaces safer and communities more livable. Instead the 1970s brought the return of inequality and the end of political support for bold social reforms.

Then the legal landscape worsened. The Supreme Court removed a potential protection against disparate environmental impacts in the form of constitutional equal protection challenges. Between 1976 and 1979, after the major environmental statutes were largely written, the Court adopted the current constitutional standard, which requires plaintiffs claiming they have been treated unequally to show that the government action they object to was affirmatively motivated by a discriminatory purpose. It isn't enough to show that, as a matter of fact, burdens are distributed in a grossly unequal way. The Constitution as interpreted by the Supreme Court doesn't care about material inequality, only whether public officials deliberately treat people differently on the basis of race or some other prohibited distinction. In other words, classic "intentional" racism in government action is unconstitutional, but what we have learned to call structural racism, the inherited material legacy of cruel and fully intended inequality, is just the way the world is. After the mid-1970s unequal harms that many thought would be open to constitutional challenge became perfectly constitutional. The antipollution statutes thus lost a critical backstop.

The other charge that today's environmental justice movement makes is that mainstream environmentalism overemphasizes elite advocacy. This, too, is not a perennial feature of environmental law, but developed in the 1970s because of specific institutional decisions. In a key part of the story, the Ford Foundation made critical investments to shape the new groups that helped to make the field of environmental law: the Environmental Law Institute, the NRDC, the Environmental Defense Fund, and others. Ford picked and cultivated its grantees to advance a vision of lawyers' role in advocacy and social reform that historians call "legal liberalism." Legal liberalism saw lawyers as channels for marginal voices that otherwise wouldn't be heard in pluralist democracy. The ideal was that if advocates could just get these marginalized voices their day in court, in front of an impartial decision maker, you could ensure that their interests were respected in the decision process. At the same time, Ford was helping to promote legal liberalism through law school clinics, ABA pro bono guidelines, and poverty law services.

The reformist goals of legal liberalism could be quite robust, but as a model of social change it had some defining limitations. It was elite driven and relied on expertise. Its advocates were inclined to imagine they spoke for a consensual "public interest" that responsible decision makers, like judges and agencies, could be trusted to pursue. And, in the end, it tied its reformist goals to the courts—at the same time that judges were retreating from their role in the 1960s as allies (if not the drivers of romantic myth) of structural change. These institutions helped to make environmentalism intensely a movement of lawyers and experts, funded by middle-class mass-membership groups and wealthy donors, and not driven by large-scale mobilization or political engagement. It took much of the fire out of a movement that had begun, on Earth Day 1970, with the largest mass mobilization in American history.

In the 1970s, as in the 1930s, there were versions of environmentalism that were less expert driven and more confrontational than those that won out. In the early 1970s, an insurgent labor organization called the Miners for Democracy briefly took over the United Mine Workers of America. They were fighting a corrupt union hierarchy that had murdered one of their leaders and his family in their home. They were pressing for safety regulations in mines that killed hundreds of people every year in disasters and thousands more slowly through black-lung disease and other industrial illnesses.

And—although this is usually forgotten even by the few people who remember them at all—they argued that if mining could not be done in an environmentally responsible way, without destroying mountains or killing streams, then miners should refuse to do it. They proposed that both safety regulations and environmental principles should be directly enforced in the workplace by strikes. Workers showed how this could go in late winter of 1969, when forty thousand miners in West Virginia walked out of the mines in a strike that all but shut down the state's coal industry until they won serious medical benefits for retirees and disabled miners dying from black-lung disease. For them, as for the 1930s activists who stood in back of Rachel Carson, the workplace and the woods and waters were all parts of the environment, and working people should defend both to defend themselves.

These ideas were not as unusual as they might have seemed later. One of the major funders of the first Earth Day was the United Auto Workers union, whose president, Walter Reuther, was a strong environmentalist who believed in using the union to advance a progressive social agenda that built on but went well beyond his members' economic interests. (Reuther also helped to fund the NAACP Legal Defense Fund, among other causes.) When he died in a plane crash in the early 1970s, he was preparing a proposal to include environmental issues in the union's collective bargaining agenda with management, so that organized labor would have been an antipollution force within the industry.

All of this is so far gone now that it is hard to recover the sense of possibility of that time. There were later tactical alliances between the new environmental groups and organized labor, especially over workplace chemical exposure, but labor never went green, and environmentalism never became a working people's movement. By 1977, the UAW opposed amendments that strengthened the Clean Air Act. On November 8, the coalfields came out strongly for Donald Trump's climate-denialist campaign, as they did in 2000 to help defeat Al Gore's environmentalist presidential candidacy.

By the early 1980s, the major environmental groups were coordinating their efforts around an agenda that put little emphasis on social and economic inequality, the disparate environmental vulnerability of marginal populations, or the special environmental threats to working people. This was the "mainstream environmentalism" that the environmental justice movement arose by criticizing. In important ways, the environmental justice advocates were right to criticize it. But few seemed to realize what a recent development it was. Ironically, the critics tended to imagine mainstream environmentalism as a perennial thing, a movement that had always been narrow in its concerns, constituency, and tactics. In the later 1980s and 1990s, it was common to describe environmentalism as the product of a narrow woods-and-waters agenda and elite constituency going all the way back to the country's origins. But even as a necessary reckoning was under way, the long environmental justice movement was lost from view.

Could things have gone differently? Maybe if supporters like Reuther, or even the Ford Foundation, had built stronger connections, say, between early environmentalism and the civil rights movement, then a greater emphasis on structural inequality, and some healthy doubts about liberal optimism, might have gone into the design of both the statutes and the institutions that came to define environmental law. If some parts of organized labor had taken militant and socially minded environmentalism into its agenda in the early 1970s and funded and supported new environmental groups alongside the liberal organizations like Ford and the wealthy donors that became the groups' lifeblood, mainstream environmentalism might have been something more like an environmental justice movement all along.

Then again, maybe not. The narrowing of the environmental agenda during the 1960s and the Ford Foundation's legal-liberal vision for advocacy were connected with the whole political economy and political culture of the United States during the Cold War. Labor's retreat into economic self-defense and zero-sum contests with environmentalists was part of a general return of inequality and scarcity in the 1970s, which affected the whole North Atlantic. The destruction of the broad egalitarian agenda that senators like Muskie expected to buttress the new environmental laws was part of a general political revolt against the twentieth-century welfare state. The structural inequality that guides environmental harms along familiar racial and class lines runs very deep.

But there are ways to retrieve the spirit of the long environmental justice movement in this time of fresh mobilization and new alliance. Environmental activists and progressive state and local governments can press for enforcement of environmental laws like the Clean Air Act and Clean Water Act in ways that are consistent with the broadly egalitarian vision that informed their creation. To give just one example, lax regulation of industrial agriculture in places like eastern North Carolina, especially the animal-feeding operations where thousands or tens of thousands of livestock are jammed together in factory-like conditions, gives the government a direct hand in exposing pervasively poor and disproportionately nonwhite people to hazardous pollutants. Aggressive enforcement of antipollution laws against facilities like these would simply make these statutes do the environmental justice work they were originally intended to do. Similarly, it was the Clean Water Act that federal district courts in southern West Virginia drew on at the turn of the millennium to declare mountaintop removal illegal. How, asked Judge Charles Haden, was it possible to protect the biological integrity of streams if they were buried under hundreds of feet and millions of tons of overburden? (In my lawyerly opinion, the appeals court in Richmond never answered the question satisfactorily, though its judges did exercise their prerogative to reverse the lower court's decision and bring mountaintop removal back within the fold of law.) There is more power and flexibility in the antipollution statutes than some of their recent uses reveal. They still have it in them to be environmental justice laws, even imperfect ones.

Environmental activists and politicians should also look for environmental injustices that are not always recognized as environmental. Consider the way that the Farm Bill, which currently pumps more than sixty-five billion dollars in subsidies into the farm economy every five years, makes calories from corn syrup and soybean oil relatively cheap and calories from healthier foods more expensive. This price skew is effectively a policy support for obesity and other diet-related diseases such as diabetes, whose prevalence is tied in turn to poverty and race. Environmentalists should see the food system as a medium of risk exposure, like air and water. The fact that eating always involves a personal choice

doesn't wash out the question of justice. Like deciding where to work, deciding what to eat is a choice
made under constraint, and the background of law
and economic inequality does a lot to define the
constraints. The members of the long environmental
justice movement, who believed the fact that your
job could make sick or kill you was no less an environmental issue because you had chosen your job,
would say the same thing today about your meal.

These are just some starting points. Other priorities may come from new allies. Maybe even the
labor movement, now both battling for its life and
being reborn in grassroots efforts like Fight for $15,
will find new points of commonality. There's no need
for environmentalists to stop being experts or to
abandon the institutions and establishment alliances
they have painstakingly built up over decades. But
they should be clear that their mission is more than
technical. They are working to defend a living world
that is under assault at every point, from the global
climate to the most vulnerable communities. Economic power, racial inequality, and the struggles of
indigenous peoples are not optional or supplemental.
They are at the heart of the work. They have always
been.

Forward

THE VALUE OF LIFE

Environmental questions are technical in many ways, but they carry us quickly toward the deepest themes. If our practical struggle is to determine who and what gets to live in the twenty-first century, how shall we shape and assess the answers? John Rawls, the great liberal political philosopher of the twentieth century, noted that these questions depend on metaphysics, a theory of the world's meaning and value and the human place in it. There is no such theory out there, just waiting for us to find it, so our environmental politics quickly becomes one that addresses the value of life. We have to struggle over nothing less.

One of the myths of our economics-minded time is that our economy contains no theory of the value of life. Instead of value, the story goes, we use the more precise and neutral concept of price—what things in fact cost. Prices, in turn, arise from the actual choices that people make in buying and selling goods and deciding how to use their time. The ways that millions of decisions weave into the prices of copper and aloe plants can be formalized mathematically, making movements in prices somewhat predictable, so the concept of price seems scientific, while value seems metaphysical. And—we're told—the concept of price respects the freedom and equality of human beings. Prices reflect people's real-life priorities in the choices they make every day. You speak your truth, I will do my thing, and our decisions will jointly produce the wage rate for the work we do, the cost of housing where we live, and the price of aloe. By contrast, a theory of value would be totalitarian. It would tell us what priorities we should have. It would amount to telling us what the meaning of our own lives should be. And isn't the point of the Declaration of Independence that your "life, liberty, and pursuit of happiness" are yours to use in your own way? Freedom and equality cannot tolerate a public theory of value, but price is their favorite child.

There are many problems with this point of view, but it remains the common sense of our time. Many of the most important environmental systems, such as the global atmosphere, are outside of prices altogether. No one agrees about how to put prices on the lives of future generations or the value of nonhuman life. Subfields of economics have been built on wrestling with these questions. Instead of calling the whole approach into doubt, these problems have been its frontiers. That is the prize of hegemony: when some obviously urgent issue is not tractable in your terms, then, like the mythic Greek robber Procrustes, you get to mutilate it until it fits into your methodological bed. The people doing this work are good, sincere, and making forms of incremental progress that can help to improve things, or at least slow their degradation. My point is not to criticize them but to point out how thoroughly even wholehearted environmental work today belongs to the dominant ways of thinking about value—that is, through the prism of price.

But there is a deep mistake here. The way we organize our world *does* contain a theory of value, and it is driving our slow but accelerating disaster for both human and nonhuman life. The world we have built imposes certain modes of value on us all. Every use of our essential human powers implies some toll on the living world, exacted through the infra-structure that is the technological exoskeleton of the species. Call your parents, travel for a family holiday, pick up food to keep yourself alive for another week, and a certain amount of fuel gets burned, a certain amount of concrete and rubber is worn down, a certain amount of soil is requisitioned for intensive production. To live as a person among other people today just is to wear down and burn up the planet by mobilizing part of your four thousand tons of technosphere. In some sense, of course, everything we do is a choice; but in another sense, we do not choose the terrible ecological terms in which these choices have their costs. We are like Saint Paul la-menting sinfulness: "What I love, I do not do; what I hate, I do." The difference is that our "sin" is the physical logic of the world we have built, and it ties what we love—communicating, being connected with other people, doing work, and taking pleasure in our short time in this world—to the harms that our living implies.

And the shape of our economy—another world we have built through the laws of property, contract, corporations, antitrust, intellectual property, employment, and the rest—imposes very direct burdens on our freedom. As the philosopher Martin Hägglund has recently reminded us, it tells us the value of our lives, cashed out in terms of the return we can produce on others' investments (or, for the very lucky, our own investments). To live has a price, in food and housing, clothing and transport, and a little pleasure. To pay that price, you must put your time and capacity up for sale. The real questions—what work is good to do, what life is good to live?—are open only at the margins, when we have paid our debts and earned our keep in this planetary workhouse. Or they are open to the lucky few. Our world, then, functions as a kind of totalitarian system of value, imposed through the mechanics of price and through the material infrastructure of our ecological interdependence and harm. It tells us the value of our own lives, and the value of life itself, of the living world. We do not really choose the uses we make of the world or of ourselves and one another. These uses are, on the whole, too exploitative, too trivial, and too mandatory. In all these senses, our systems betray the ideas they supposedly uphold, of the equality and freedom of human beings. They impose a flawed and destructive theory of value, which deforms our power *really* to choose the terms of our relations to one another and to the nonhuman world. This deforming theory of value is built into our material and economic infrastructures. We have made a world that overmasters us. Some of us have learned to call it freedom, and others call it sin. But the reality is both worse and better than that. It is the sum of human choices and powers, and those—only those—can remake it.

These are the terms in which a commonwealth is possible: a way of living in which our survival and flourishing do not prey constantly and involuntarily on the lives of others, in which, instead, my flourishing is the condition of your flourishing, and yours reciprocally of mine. To build a commonwealth means a deep reworking of two intertwined infrastructures, the economy and the material technosphere. If we change those, we will have changed human nature and begun a kind of peace with one another and the rest of life.

Let's make this idea more concrete. The deep thing in the idea of a Green New Deal is the recognition that, in the Anthropocene, remaking the economy and remaking our relation to ecology are two sides of the same change. The planet's fate is written in how we make our energy, dispose of our waste, and value our lives. The transformation would, first, make work to remake a world—the work of infrastructure building for carbon-neutral energy, transport, heat and cooling—a transformation of the technosphere to make us into a species that belongs here. This would be a jobs program, and people sometimes sneer at that idea. But the Department of Homeland Security with a quarter million employees, is a jobs program. The quarter trillion dollars that the Defense Department spent on private contractors in Iraq and Afghanistan between 2007 and 2017 was a jobs program. The number of American jobs that exist because we continue to tolerate—and subsidize—the oil and gas industry is at least 1.4 million or, if you believe an industry-funded study from 2017, over 10 million. Energy infrastructure and government are jobs programs by their nature. The question is what kind of work they make—and what kind of world. The infrastructure we need, which today's market will not build, is the kind that will decouple our human powers, our communication and work and care, our moving and building, everything we do, from the exhaustion of the planet. Our living should instead support the constant renewal of the living world. That means a different economy of energy.

That idea of a world-renewing ecological commonwealth is a key to another idea: an economy that prizes the work of sustaining and renewing the human world. Such an economy would prize nurses comparably to surgeons and more than the investors who buy up medical patents in speculation. It would reward elementary and high school teachers comparably to professors at research universities, and more than the companies whose engineers design addictive products to increase the sum of human needs, whether drugs or soft-blue screens. This change would upend the logic of the labor market and replace its bottom line with different purposes. Today we are locked into making ourselves instruments of one another's profits, with some lucky ones finding spaces of exemption where they are able to pursue other values, or overlap where their work coincides with something they believe intrinsically good. In a commonwealth economy, we should root ourselves in helping the world, human and natural, to go on being.

Everyone knows this. There are no secrets here. We are suffering not from ignorance or innocence but from a lack of faith that understanding can help us. It is ordinary now to say, maybe as an aside, that things are pretty much over, that we are just waiting for the end. It's meant as a mark of sophistication, and also a kind of "don't blame me!" Its effect is creepingly nihilistic. If you believe this—and I suspect most of us believe it at least partly and at least some of the time, because so much in our lives bespeaks it—then you are waiting for the end of the world. Maybe you are hoping to amass enough wealth or cultural capital that your grandchildren will be among the ones who keep a leg up in a world of refugees, resource wars, and extreme weather, the ones who control the fertile fields and clean water, or a piece of high ground in a possibly stable redoubt such as New Zealand. Maybe you are just hoping that things don't get too bad while you are still young enough to take pleasure in life.

I can hardly fault anyone for believing these things today, when the evidence for despair is so weighty and clear. But as I write, another impulse is also rising. If the problem is the world we have built, then it is in our power to build another. To make a safer, stabler world, we will have to shake the pillars of this one. It will take great acts of democratic will to say what is valuable for us, what we want to orient our entire built world toward cultivating and preserving: the unbroken flow of life and caregiving, human and nonhuman. In a commonwealth—which we might also call a democratic Anthropocene—value will lie in work that does what is necessary and sustains its own conditions of possibility, in rest that contemplates a broken but still wondrous world, in play that keeps joy vivid among monuments and ruins and helps ensure that new life will grow there. No one can choose these values alone because they depend on the shared commitments of others and on the shape and terms of a built and shared world. The heroic work of building that world must clear the space for living humbly. We need extraordinary acts to serve the most common things. It will seem less heroic, more ordinary, if it is the work of many hands, and that is the only way it will come true.

Index